Young Person's
BECOMING A

Other Books by Janet E. Grant:

The Writing Coach

Lifechoices: A Personal and Career Life Management Guide (Co-authored with Judith Campbell and Fred French)

The Kids' Green Plan: How to Make Your Own Plan to Save the Environment

Kids' Writers: Dennis Lee, Lucy Maud Montgomery, Jean Little and Bob Munsch

Madeleine de Vercheres

Canadians All 6: Portraits of Our People (Co-authored with Alistair Sweeney)

Canadians All 5: Portraits of Our People (Co-authored with Fred Sass and Doris Cowan)

Young Person's Guide to
BECOMING A WRITER

JANET E. GRANT

SHOE TREE PRESS
WHITE HALL, VIRGINIA

Published by Shoe Tree Press, an imprint of
Betterway Publications, Inc.
P.O. Box 219
Crozet, VA 22932
(804) 823-5661

Cover design and photograph by Susan Riley
Typography by Park Lane Associates

Library of Congress Cataloging-in-Publication Data

Grant, Janet
  Young person's guide to becoming a writer / Janet E. Grant.
    p. cm.
  Includes index.
Summary: Advice on improvement exercises, experimenting with
techniques, character sketches, setting up a schedule, identifying
strengths, getting published, money, helpful organizations, and
more.
  ISBN 1-55870-215-6 : $8.95
  1. Children as authors. 2. Authorship--Handbooks, manuals,
etc.--Juvenile literature. [1. Authorship--Handbooks, manuals, etc.]
  I. Title.
PN171.C5G68 1991
808'.02--dc20   91-19473
                                                               CIP
                                                                AC

Printed in the United States of America
0 9 8 7 6 5 4 3 2 1

With love to my very special parents,
Enid and Terry Grant.

Acknowledgments

To my father for placing in my hands upon graduation, *What Color Is Your Parachute*, thanks for always being there to listen to my ideas. To my mother, for her love of tennis and for showing by example that you always make room for the next generation.

My thanks to I.M. Pfaff, my high school teacher, who saved my life by suggesting that I study at a university in England, and to Larry Lerner, my professor in English Literature, and the faculty at Sussex University for teaching a program that truly inspired the students to think for themselves.

To two highly-respected nonfiction authors, Richard N. Bolles and Tony Buzan, a profound thank you for the wealth of knowledge in your books, which I read over ten years ago and I still use today. To Tom McKeown, president of Clear Communication Consultations, who saw me "mind-mapping" one day, and decided I should be trained to lead corporate seminars, and to Ian McClelland, the editor at Methuen who gave me my first break into publishing, I will always be grateful.

The young writers and the staff of the 1989 and 1990 Canadian Young Authors' Camp contributed in their own special way to the relevance of the material of this book. Special thanks to: Aric Green for caring so much about horror stories; Adam Bekhor for his keen insight and humor; and Angie Kays, John Greig, Zahra Sachedina, Steve Martin, Christine Carriere, and Peter Martin for contributing articles for this book.

Many authors and staff at various writing organizations in Canada, the United States, Great Britain, Australia, and Sweden shared their insights and experiences and what they would do if they could do it over again. In particular, thanks to Hazel Edwards, Nazneen Sadiq, Kathy Henderson, Kerstin Backman, Penny Dickens, Mark Thurman, and George Swede.

To my long-time friends, Catriona Troth, Monica Evans, Natalie Gold, Barbara Annis, Jeanine Fisher, Kathy Lazowski, Joan Gibbons, and Julia and John Page, thanks for your encouragement and understanding when I disappeared for months on end to write.

A final thanks to my brothers, Ian and Alan, and my sisters, Jennifer and Judith, for all the love and the laughs!

Preface

A WORD TO YOUNG WRITERS

In America only the successful writer is important, in France all writers are important, in England no writer is important, and in Australia you have to explain what a writer is.
  Geoffrey Cotterell

When I was fifteen, I had a strong interest in writing. I kept a diary every year and wrote some poetry. But most of my writing was still for school assignments. I wanted to write a novel. I had a couple of false starts, and then went back to doing what I knew I do best — reading books and playing tennis.

Nearly twenty years later, I have written the *Young Person's Guide to Becoming a Writer* to give young writers around the world a real sense of how to develop their own writing talent and make the most of the years between the ages twelve and twenty-four.

You may know right now that writing is all you ever want to do. On the other hand, you may want to write part-time as you pursue another career that is equally important. Some young people just naturally grow into being writers.

I didn't decide at fifteen to become a writer. I decided at fifteen that I would like to change the way teenagers were educated. My career as a writer of nonfiction books and director of the International Young Authors' Camps has come as a result of that.

Being a writer inspires me. I have the freedom to establish my own hours—if the sun is shining I can go out and play; I can produce a piece of work to my own level of satisfaction; and I feel I am making a valuable contribution to society.

Becoming a writer is both a mysterious and magical process. It is a lifetime journey that takes roots in your early childhood with the reading of books, unfolds as you learn to write in your teen years, and then unleashes itself—driven by your imagination and determination.

May you become the writer of your dreams!

Preface

A WORD TO PARENTS AND TEACHERS

As both young writers and parents suspect, there are many things young writers can be doing to enable them to become better writers. As you watch the young writer in your home or classroom devour books at an astonishing rate (yes, even after you've switched off the bedroom light, there's a flashlight at work), it is only natural to wonder if there is something more they can be doing than simply reading and writing school assignments.

Most young writers, their parents, and their teachers are looking for suggestions on how to help develop their writing talent. As Director of the International Young Authors' Camps, I receive phone calls and letters daily, requesting help.

Young Person's Guide to Becoming a Writer is written for any young writer (ages twelve to twenty-four) who wants to really understand what it takes to become a writer. This is not a creative writing book that attempts to analyze the magic behind the creative writing process. It is a book with an innovative method for coaching young writers. It helps all young writers to look at their skills, their weaknesses, the types of writing they do best, and the amount of time they want to spend writing in order to teach them to become their own writing experts.

Young Person's Guide to Becoming a Writer also includes

essential information on getting published, how a writer gets paid, finding other young writers, having a manuscript evaluated, getting support from parents and teachers, and how to make a sensible career decision. Each young writer is encouraged to develop at her own pace and according to her own values and goals.

The coaching method is at the heart of the extraordinary success of the Canadian Young Authors' Camp, which attracts young adults from across North America and authors from around the world.

While the challenges in this book may surprise you, in my experience young adults have an extraordinary energy, curiosity, and desire for authentic information. (Isn't their favorite question: "How is it going to be of help to me after I leave school?")

Becoming a writer takes time. It is an extraordinary journey that can start in those teenage years. With this book in hand, young writers can avoid repeating the mistakes generation upon generation of writers have made before them, and put their energy into writing the literature so essential to society.

Table of Contents

*All natural or born writers are possessed,
and in the old magical sense, by their own
imaginations long before they even
began to think of writing.*

John Fowles

Chapter 1

The Land of the Imagination

You are sitting by a river daydreaming. The river sounds a particular way. Before you know it, you are transported into another world where the sound of the river is not just a sound, it is anything you dare to make it. You can transform it. You can re-create it. Each time, you do it a little differently.

You are walking home in the evening after being with a friend. The full moon is out. You remember the moon is not just a moon. In the land of the imagination, it is the place a cow jumped over. It is a place where the man in the moon lives. You look up again at the moon, and one image or many images come into your mind. You play with the one that fits best. You put words to it. You repeat those words to yourself, then let them slip away. Or you carefully take them home with you and record them in a journal.

Just as the artist learns to draw by seeing the space around an object, rather than just the object, the writer learns to write by seeing what is not there, and then imagining what could be there. For when writers play with their imaginations, they are playing with the truth. We can make our own anything in the world and everything not in it. To be played with, captured, transformed, and re-created. Such are the extraordinary laws of imagination.

When people are really aware of the magic of the creative imagination, they feel as if they can walk through walls! Johnathon, age fourteen, describes it as "an escape from the present world, into a world that's all my own. Mine to create as I want it. A world where I call the shots and make the rules." Sigrid, age thirteen, says, "I love writing because it gives me a chance for my imagination to go wild."

The young person who loves to write is just entering that stage of being able to tap in and out of the land of the imagination. You already like to write and imagine things. It may not be very easy to see why or how. That's just fine. Learning to see why you write or how you write is part of becoming a writer.

HOW DO YOU KNOW IF YOU ARE A WRITER?

There are signs. Perhaps when you do the ink blot test (a test in which you are given an ink blot and asked to come up with as many things as you see it could be), you cover two sides of the page.

Or you daydream without a problem. Bob Munsch, a Canadian author and storyteller extraordinaire, says he daydreamed all the time as a young man, especially in the classroom.

Or perhaps you keep a diary to record events, people, and feelings. Lucy Maud Montgomery, creator of *Anne of Green Gables*, wrote in her diary every day from the age of nine. She felt that not to write daily in her diary would be as bad as not washing her face!

Taking the Same Steps

All over the world, young writers take similar steps in starting their careers. As one young writer in Washington, DC jumps for joy because her first article has been accepted for publication, another writer in the Lake District of England looks proudly at his poem in a local magazine. As one young writer walks home from school in Montreal, Canada, discouraged by the fact that there is no other person his age to talk with about writing, another young writer in Melbourne, Australia takes a biography of a famous writer off the library shelves as a substitute for a companion. As one young writer in Copenhagen, Denmark picks up his pen to write a story and stops because the main character is suddenly misbehaving, another young writer in Amsterdam, Holland finds that the plot of her story has turned boring almost overnight.

Special Concerns

Young writers who wish to develop their own writing talent have their own special set of concerns and needs. As avid readers, they are eager to find more challenging books. Comfortable with expressing themselves on paper, they are ready to do practical exercises to bring new depths to their writing. Ready to make new friends who also share an interest in writing, they are willing to seek out unusual opportunities to meet other young writers who may be younger or older than they are. Faced inevitably with making a first career decision, they need a simple explanation of how a writer makes enough money to earn a living, along with other information about the day-to-day realities of being a writer.

FOUR AREAS FOR DEVELOPING YOUR WRITING TALENT

Benjamin S. Bloom has written a book entitled, *Developing Talent in Young People*. He states: "All the talented individuals we interviewed invested considerable practice and training time, which rivalled the time devoted to school or any other activity. And this time in many ways was more intense and rewarding than the time they put into almost anything else."

All young writers know instinctively that reading books is one way to develop their abilities as writers. But besides reading, and perhaps writing occasionally, it is not particularly clear what else they should do.

Yet if you play a competitive sport after school, you already are familiar with drills and the idea of practicing one's skills. If you have attended art classes, you know you can look around for special classes and instructors. In fact, you can use your experience in just about any other field (e.g., sports and the arts) to help you become a writer.

Look at your friends with interests in piano, hockey, tennis, or skiing. They have drills or practices to do. They work with coaches. They sometimes even give recitals or perform in competitions.

Perhaps some of these things could be adapted for writing. Perhaps the steps to becoming a writer are not that mysterious after all!

Ask yourself the following questions:

1. Has anyone encouraged you to find out what kind of writing you have a natural tendency for?
2. Has anyone shown you ways to develop characters and plots?
3. Has anyone encouraged you to write regularly each day?
4. Has anyone encouraged you to find a mentor?
5. Has anyone advised you to join a writing club or writing organization?

Over the years of working with young writers (both in schools and privately), I have found that there are four areas young writers can work on which will help them improve their writing significantly.

Schedule regular writing times and use that time wisely. How? Schedule a regular writing time that fits in with your timetable. What should you do with this time? Learn to expand your observation powers and imagination. Play with settings, characters, words, and storyboards. The way you see the world is unique. But are you getting your best writing down on paper?

Learn about different types of writing. How? Understand the structure of the genres you are working in. Learn how the genres have developed over the years. Do you ever wonder why you can't seem to write anything longer than a short story? Or why your plays sound like documentaries? Or why you always seem to write only one kind of poetry?

Surround yourself with good support. How? Get feedback on your work. Have someone to talk with or write to about writing. Figure out the best support network for you. Find out about young writers' clubs, mentors, pen pals, and special writing classes and camps with professional authors.

Understand the publishing industry. How? Learn about the publishing industry and how it works. You can improve your chances of being published. Learn to avoid the most common mistakes novice writers make starting out in their careers.

As a writer, you can give yourself writing practice time. You can go to writing classes, find your own writing coach or mentor, read from your work at special reading nights, and enter writing competitions. You can develop your writing talent!

If you could have changed one thing in your youth, what would it be?

I would have changed my classmates.
Jean Little

I would have believed more in my dreams.
Jean Booker

I wish I had read even more widely and in at least one other language than English.
Isabel Huggan

THIS BOOK

This book is meant to empower you. In this case, my intention is to empower you to become the best writer possible. Each chapter contains specific information that helps you avoid the most common mistakes both young and old writers make. Each chapter also contains challenging activities that call upon some of the things young writers like doing best: reading and researching information.

I suggest that you use a notebook in which to record your responses to these activities. Write down your responses plus any insights you discover about yourself. The activities will help you fine-tune all the necessary skills of being a writer for years to come. You may find it useful to review certain chapters in a year or two's time. Remember that by keeping focused on what you really want and fine-tuning your ideas regularly, you will achieve what you want.

Here are some words that may be new to you.

Insight. The word "insight" means to see something familiar in a new way so you can take new action on it. Or you may be more familiar with saying to yourself, "Aha! I know now why I was doing that. Now I can choose to do this instead." Write your insights down as you work through this book.

Commitment. By the word "commitment" I mean the degree to which you care about your writing and want to learn and nurture your writing ability. For example, every year I screen young writers for the Canadian Young Authors' Camp held in Haliburton, Canada, according to their commitment to their writing. Who am I to say what is possible for a young writer at the age of eleven to nineteen? I know what is possible, but what that young writer will actually do is up to her. For as life has shown, time and time again, the talent must be coupled with a commitment. That is because it is the commitment that will keep you going in the right direction.

Declaration. A declaration is a statement that creates a whole new reality. For example, when John F. Kennedy said we would put a man on the moon before the end of the century, he was making a declaration. He had no real firm evidence. He just said he would do it.

You are a writer by your own declaration. It is a bit like putting the cart before the horse. Most people wait until their first book or article is published to declare that they are writers. They wait for the evidence. Try declaring that you are a writer (if that is true for you) and then watch what happens.

Declarations are very powerful.

✎_____**ACTIVITIES**

Four Areas for Developing Your Writing Talent

Think for a moment of what you have done up to now to develop your writing ability. Have you written as much as you have wanted? Have you really given yourself a chance to explore writing different stories? Have you managed to find some friends who also write? Do you know anything about the publishing industry?

Take your notebook and write at the top of the first page, "Four Areas to Work on to Become a Writer."

Rate yourself with the appropriate number for each of the four talent areas below — '3' for well-developed, '2' for okay, and '1' for undeveloped. If a really good idea comes to you about how you could improve in one of these areas, then jot it down in your notebook. (There are activities and suggestions on how to improve in all four areas throughout this book.)

- Schedule regular writing time and use that time wisely.
- Learn about different types of writing.
- Surround yourself with good support for your writing.
- Understand the publishing industry.

An Afternoon with Your Favorite Authors

While it would be nice to meet all our favorite authors in person, sometimes it just is not possible. They may live far away from us. They may have lived one hundred years ago! But that doesn't mean that you can't read about them in reference books.

Think of three writers whom you would like to know more about. Go to your local library and ask the librarian to help you find biographies, autobiographies, or short biographical sketches on the three authors.

In Canada and the U.S. a good place to start is the two titles given below. They are a series of volumes that contain fascinating short references to authors from all countries. First, *Authors & Artists for Young Adults*, edited by Agnes Garrett and Helga P. McCue (Detroit: Gale Research Inc., 1989). Second, *Yesterday's Authors of Books for Children*, by Ann Commire (Detroit: Gale Research Inc., 1977). In Australia, you can read *No Kidding* by Agnes Neuenhausen (Chippendale: Macmillan/Pen, 1991) and *Storymakers 1 and 2* by Margaret Dunkle (Oxford: Oxford University Press).

Then, find a comfortable armchair and curl up for the afternoon. You may find some interesting similarities and dissimilarities between you and your favorite writers!

To find out more about how talent development occurs with young people your own age, try reading: Benjamin Bloom's *Developing Talent in Young People* (New York: Ballantine, 1985). Once you have finished reading it, pass it on to your parents. After finishing this book, you can sit down with your parents or a favorite teacher and discuss how they can help you.

Chapter 2
Identifying the Young Writer Within

Those who know others are intelligent;
Those who know themselves have insight.
Those who master others have force;
Those who master themselves have strength.
  Tao Te Ching, R.L. Wing (translator)

Taking time to step aside and think about the world is what makes us all writers. We write in response to the events happening around us, the people talking around us, or the social events shaping the planet. But we also need to take time to look at ourselves. Why do I write? What exactly am I trying to say to others? These are very powerful questions to ask. A powerful question doesn't have just one answer. A powerful question means we could spend our whole lives answering it. By living in a question, you may come up with an answer one day and come up with an even clearer one next week.

What makes you different from the writers in your class? What makes you or your writing different from any other person in your school? And if you've had your writing published in your community, what makes you different from, say, the lady who writes down the street or the local reporter who writes sports stories? What makes you different from Roald Dahl, Bob Munsch, J.R.R. Tolkien, Cynthia Voigt, Isaac Asimov, Astrid Lindgren, Paul Jennings, or any other writer for that matter?

Each writer has his own style of writing. Who you are plays an important role in your writing: the types of writing you like doing best, the problems you set up for your characters to solve, your choice of settings, and even the imagery in your poetry.

MY WRITING PHILOSOPHY, OR THE REASON I WRITE

The reasons young people write are as varied as the young people themselves. You see yourself as an individual with a unique or personalized response for doing things.

Young writers like to somehow make sense of what is happening to them in day-to-day life, i.e., sometimes through expressing emotions. Young writers like to use writing as a means of escape. (This type of "escaping" isn't bad at all. It is a healthy exercising of the imagination.) Young writers like to use writing as a vehicle for communicating important information, either a story or a series of thoughts. Affecting the reader by either entertaining or teaching him is an important motive in writing. These motives are also the driving force behind many well-known authors, too.

I stress the significance of life before twenty-one. I don't look at my characters' childhoods as a time for growth and development or as a carefree interlude until one is forced to enter the real world in later life. This is the real world full of powerful friendships, strong values, fears, triumphs and failures.

Gordon Korman,
a popular author of young adult novels

If the book we are reading does not wake us, as with a fist hammering on the skull, then why do we read it? . . . A book must be like an ice-axe to break the sea frozen inside us.

Franz Kafka

I like to express my feelings, stretch my imagination, and earn money.

Susan E. Hinton, who wrote The Outsiders

Others' Writing Philosophies

As you read through these philosophies by other young writers your own age, watch for the clues as to what that young writer is concerned about. There are hints of the characters they want to write about, the problems that intrigue them, the importance of working with their imagination, and the need for expressing emotional concerns.

To me writing is a means of self-expression as well as a means of escaping from reality into a world of fantasy, discovery, and tranquillity . . . To be sensitive towards the environment is the philosophy behind good writing.
Zahra, fifteen

I believe that children have new ideas to share but lack the experience to express themselves. In between two worlds are the young adults who should be given a chance to teach the world untarnished values. If they succeed, the world becomes better. If they fail, they will learn and try again.
Derek, eighteen

In the world we live in today, there is a lack of imagination. People are very scientific. You have to use imagination to give a different perspective of the world.
Dave, fourteen

My work is a reflection of my life and events in it. It keeps me from punching walls. It allows me to release the ideas which get caught in my head, leaving my mind stuck in a perpetual 'rinse' cycle.
Jessie, seventeen

I want my readers to feel everything I've put into my writing and I want them to feel close to my characters. I want to leave an impression. And I don't want to make people laugh or cry; I want them to do both.
Liz, sixteen

The ordinary person, the one who is not readily noticed, the person who is not full of Hollywood glitter and glitz . . . this is the character who brings forth the real revelation of life.
Christine, nineteen

I want to make the impossible believable. I want to make people look over their backs. If that means scaring them, all the better. I want to educate and entertain by bringing the surreal to people's front door. If nothing else, they must almost believe what I say, and be affected. I must leave my mark.
Peter, fifteen

Let's take the last example, Peter's, to look just briefly at what philosophies can tell you. What are some of the clues you think Peter's writing philosophy is signaling? What type of stories do you think he writes? If you guessed thriller/horror — you're right! He is also asking for his readers to give him feedback that he has indeed made the impossible believable. He is willing to dig deep into his characters' motives.

KNOWING YOUR PRECISE SKILLS

It is the moment, if you will, when a Little Leaguer discovers, not that he or she can pitch (which he/she may have known for some time), but that he or she has a particular ability to throw the good live fastball or to pop a curve that rises or dips outrageously.

Stephen King, Danse Macabre

Often as young writers develop they have a magical moment where they realize there is one particular thing they do very well. In fact, they do it so well, it is a unique talent. This is part of the process of growing up—exploring and finding out what you do well.

Does your writing show that you are highly imaginative? Are your descriptions of people so sensitive that it shows you are an alert observer of people? Does your sense of humor make people laugh?

The skills you demonstrate in your writing are one way of cluing into your own particular ability as a writer. Richard N. Bolles, a career counselor and author of *What Color is Your Parachute*, advises people to look for work that includes their favorite skills. While thinking in terms of skills may be totally new to you, it allows you to be more inventive in both your writing and career choices.

The Top Ten Skills

Out of all the skills one develops as a writer, I have compiled a list of what I think are the ten most important *all-round* skills. As you read through the list, you won't be surprised to see reading and writing on the list. But you most likely will be surprised to see computer skills and financial planning on the list. The term "financial planning" is something you may have heard your parents or other adults talking about.

The point is to read through this list to inform yourself about the skills needed. You may want to read through the list two or three times. This is a list that you can *grow* with and gradually learn to *master*.

You are not expected to have all these skills right now or even when you graduate. They are skills that you will work on and refine all through your life. Each skill is discussed in the following chapters of this book; for example, project planning is discussed in Chapter 4 and financial planning is discussed in Chapter 7.

1. Writing. Your writing shows that you know how to spell, you have a good sense of choosing the right words, and you use proper grammar. Your writing may show a certain flair—humor, character description, twist endings, etc. Your writing has a unique style of its own. You are not afraid to learn and try out new words.

2. Reading. You look for good books all the time. As you grow each year, you look for new books, perhaps award-winning books, books written by local authors, and even books written by authors in other countries. You enjoy reading different types of books and magazines.

3. Observing. You take the time to observe people accurately. You take in the details of what they are wearing, how they are standing, what they are saying, and their body language. You are always noticing things and training your eye to capture both usual and unusual items that can be used in your settings.

4. Imagination. You have a well-developed imagination. You love to play with ideas and events in your mind. You can create characters and characters' names very quickly—almost like a game. You like to invent scenarios in which characters are talking to each other. You can almost see the characters right in front of you. You understand that you can use your imagination for both fiction and nonfiction projects.

5. Project Planning. You are good at planning. You have a realistic idea of how many pages you want a writing project to be. You know your own writing habits and can plan to deliver a project on time. You understand that running past deadlines doesn't work in publishing any more than it does at school.

6. Research. You are able to find facts — even unusual ones—to support your historical stories, to provide the basis of a plot in your science fiction story, and to find the best publisher. At best, you work quickly and effectively.

7. Initiative. When it comes to things that are important to you, you are clear on what you want to get done and you take steps to do it. You are able to ask people to help you to do things when you don't know how. You keep finding ways to get things done even if problems keep cropping up. You don't wait for someone to tell you to do something.

8. Persuasion. You are able to persuade people about the merit of doing a project or doing something important in your life.

9. Typing and Computer Skills. You can type over

forty words a minute. You are able to operate a computer, including a word-processing program and a spreadsheet program.

10. Financial Planning. You are able to write up your own simple budget. You make sensible financial goals and spend your money wisely. You have learned how writers get paid.

_____**ACTIVITIES**

Writer's Bluff

How well do you really know your favorite writer? Pretend for a moment that you have been given a page of writing from one of your favorite writers. Neither the title nor the writer of the book is on the page. The characters' names (if any) have been blotted out.

How could you identify your favorite writer? Does he write in a particular way, or write about a special subject? Now, try another favorite writer, poet, or playwright. Again, what would be the telltale clue that would identify her?

After a while you should be able to tell different writers apart, just as you can tell different rock groups or classical composers apart.

With some imagination and preparation, you can make this into a game to play with writing and reading friends.

The Reason You Write

Why do you think you write? Have you ever tried to express why you write by actually writing it down? You may know your reasons right away; you may need to think about them. Here are some questions to help you.

1. What do you want your readers to be left with when they read your writing? (A new understanding of how important relatives are? To laugh at your jokes?)
2. What makes certain books important to you? (They make you learn things? They express ideas you care about?)
3. How do you see the role of books in a society's development? (Entertainment? Education? Reflecting what society can't see?)

In your notebook, write a sentence or two of your own reason(s) for writing. You can call this your *writing philosophy*. As time passes, you should also look back at your philosophy and consider whether it has changed in any way. Record these changes also.

My Writing Philosophy Is:

To make the reader ask questions of himself.
It is a challenge in a world which, without these questions, would quickly stagnate.

Revision (1 year later)
To make the young adults question their role in society.
To make use of real events rather than science fiction.

Know Your Precise Skills

Here is a short list of skills—by no means all of them—a writer may use.

- Be highly imaginative.
- Think new and unusual thoughts.
- Write detailed descriptions of people.
- Use symbolism.
- Listen for the correct dialogue.
- Have a good sense of humor.
- Proofread for correct spelling and grammar.
- Be willing to rewrite until the best writing possible is produced.
- Be patient.
- Be curious.
- Influence the attitudes of people.
- Write about sensitive personal matters.
- Reason persuasively.

You may think of other skills that are valuable to writers in general, or more specifically, to yourself as a writer. Jot these down in your notebook.

Consider which skills you feel you have already. Write down the ones you enjoy. You may also want to make note of those skills you feel weak in, but are important enough for you to work at improving them. Become familiar with this list of skills so that you can help your friends identify their own sets of skills. The combination of any of these skills should give you a clearer idea of where your writing strengths lie.

What Do They Really Mean When They Say . . .

How many times have you heard: "You are a good writer"; "Keep on writing, you have talent"; "That was a good essay"; or "You should take English at the university since you love to read so much"?

You've politely said, "Thank you," only to wonder, seconds later, what it really was they liked about your writing. By learning about different skills a writer has, you can start to listen for which particular skills the person might be complimenting you on.

If you have received any of the following four compliments, consider which skills listed below them you think the person was referring to. You may come up with your own skills that are not listed.

You are a gifted writer!
- You are original in a particular area of writing (character descriptions, setting, dialogue, etc.).
- You are able to follow detailed instructions.
- You prioritize tasks well.
- You complete tasks on time.
- You see the relationship between different factors.

You wrote a wonderful story!
- You are highly imaginative.
- You are an alert observer of people.

You write good letters.
- You express yourself well.
- You describe people and scenes vividly.
- You employ humor in describing experiences.

You wrote a great essay!
- You have a memory for details.
- You are able to compare information.
- You communicate clearly.

In your notebook, write down two compliments you have received in the past about your writing ability. Then write down the skills you think you were actually demonstrating when you were complimented.

1. Compliment: Your story was very funny!
   Skills: humor, character descriptions
2. Compliment: What a story! I never expected the unusual ending.
   Skills: building suspense, well thought out plot

The next time you receive a compliment about your writing, you can use your knowledge of skills to discover what the person is really saying. If you want a clearer statement, you can prompt the person with specific questions.

Here are a few examples:

Reader: I really liked your piece.
Writer: Oh really, thank you. What did you like in particular?
Reader: The way you described that village. I felt like I was right there.
Reader: I really liked the way you started your story.
Writer: Oh, that's interesting. What did you find pleasing about it?
Reader: It was a strong symbol of life, and you played upon that image until the end of the story.

Rate Your Basic Skills

In the example is a list of ten skills that can be powerful tools in your writing. As the young writer has done in this example, try copying the list in your notebook, and then honestly rating yourself on these skills. A '3' can stand for good; '2' for adequate; and '1' for undeveloped. As you work on your writing, consider those skills you rated yourself adequate or undeveloped on, and come up with ways you can improve in these areas.

	Skill	Demonstrated Ability
1.	Writing	2
2.	Reading	3
3.	Observing	3
4.	Imagination	3
5.	Project Planning	2
6.	Research	1
7.	Initiative	3
8.	Persuasion	2
9.	Typing and Computer Skills	1
10.	Financial Skills	1

Note to improve:
Research — ?
Typing and Computer Skills — Take Computer course at school next year.
Financial Skills — Take accounting Course at school when it is offered.

Reading

To find out more about skills, read some of the following books.

Bolles, Richard Nelson. *What Color Is Your Parachute?* Berkeley: Ten Speed Press. (Published annually.)

This book is so good, it is updated and published annually. If you have to make a career decision soon, read and do the exercises in this book on a school break. If you don't have to make a career decision soon, read the introduction.

Buzan, Tony. *Use Your Head*. Ariel. London: 1974.

This book has sold over 1,000,000 copies and been translated into many languages. This is the book I wished someone had given me before I went to university. You will never look at a stack of books the same way again.

Chapter 3

Writing What You Write Best

Recently this year I would sit down to write, and the feeling I would get was one of 'You have two choices: a) scratch off a short, disastrous poem or b) try writing a story where you always stop in the middle of it.'

Jaylene, sixteen

There is a unique opportunity for young writers who really understand the different types of writing so that they can choose the ones they write best.

What type of writing do you write best? How can you write better poetry? What do you do when you get stuck? How many pages should a short story be?

All these questions and more can be answered by examining the art form of genres you are interested in. Different types of writing are called genres. There is a wide variety of writing genres.

By learning how different genres were started and have developed over the years, plus some of the "rules" (which can be broken), you can learn what writing you do best.

THE WIDE WORLD OF GENRES

Young Writers Talk about Genres

One of the requirements of being at the Canadian Young Authors' Camp has been for young writers to write a piece about something important they learned while at camp. For a majority of the writers, learning about genres was very important. As Cara, age eighteen, said about the camp, "By being surrounded by people who specialize in different genres, I learned that there is a place for all kinds of writing."

Here are four articles about genres. The views contained in these pieces are those of the young writers. The pieces are simple enough to give you a sense of the genre, plus get a preview of some of the things you should be thinking about if you are writing in that genre.

"The Picture Book"

by Zahra Sachedina

Picture books are a pleasurable yet challenging literary art form. Having become number one favorites among children, many have earned a permanent place within the heart of the young.

I can still remember myself as a young child opening up a picture book and simply adoring the myriad of colors that sprung out before me from each page! In fact, this sensation lit a spark within me, nurturing my fascination with picture books and encouraging me to focus on writing for children.

The stepping stone that uncovered hidden talents I didn't know existed was a grade seven assignment in which I was asked to write and illustrate and hand-bind a picture book. I developed a strong sense for art as I continued creating these handmade books. Soon, I realized that my stories had begun to take shape years before I actually wrote them. They were composed of small incidents from my childhood; almost like photographs of memorable moments. The secret to good writing had been unlocked . . . writing about what I knew best.

Many young authors overlook this genre as it is not as well recognized as poetry writing or short story writing. The following guidelines may be considered when writing picture books.

1. Begin by choosing an age group you wish to write for. Follow this age guide to help you put your story into perspective.
2. Explore your genre fully; that is, read what other picture book authors have written to gain a solid foundation.

3. Write and edit a rough draft. Have someone else read it for a second opinion.

4. If you wish to illustrate your story, plan your pictures and text on a storyboard before you start the actual illustrations.

5. Transfer the storyboard ideas onto your final copy and complete it with detailed illustrations. You may wish to bind the book for a professional finish.

One of the main things to remember is that the book should be read aloud, and therefore try to develop a rhythm/rhyme scheme throughout the story in order to maintain a sense of oral imagery.

"Playwriting"

by Angie Kays

Often playwriting is overlooked as a possible genre for young writers. As you look over your own writing, there are clues that suggest a possible strength for writing drama. Does your dialogue run on for pages and pages in a seemingly endless flow? Do you attach more importance to what your characters say and how they say it than to any other element of your stories? Does your description of settings and characters' actions read like stage directions? When you write, do you visualize your work being performed?

Through my experience of having my plays "workshopped" (produced on stage and directed with professional help), I have learned a lot about writing plays. For example:

1. *Always be listening.* In restaurants, on buses, constantly listen so that natural dialogue seeps into your subconsciousness and then pours out freely in your writing. Observe people, not only for what they say, but also for what they don't say. Often theater is the motion behind the thought; it's the equivalent of reading between the lines in literature.

2. *Use an outline.* Dialogue has a funny way of getting stuck in one place; a plot outline helps keep dialogue flowing smoothly and advancing through the beginning, middle, and end of your piece.

3. *Keep your characters distinct.* Give each one a unique vocabulary and a favorite expression. Just as all of us have different speech patterns in real life, characters in plays should

as well.

Finally, read. Read Chekhov, Aristophanes, Moliére, and Fennario. Devour the imagery of Shakespeare. Most of all, never ever stifle the conversations that go on in your head. They can be some of the most powerful material for your plays!

"Writing for the Children's Market: Children Ages 8-12"

by Jaylene Rashleigh

I came with the idea that I wrote for young adults and no one else. As it turns out, I'm also interested in children's books. I suppose the fact that I really like working with primary children and watching them learn has brought this fact out. Before I had never really thought about writing children's books.

The easiest part of writing for young children is that it is so simplistic. Your imagination really has no limits to what you wish to write or how you wish to present it. If you are lucky enough to be near children as I am, the situations you are pulled into with them are usually rich in ideas and plots. And, you can find stories in everyday routines or situations: babysitting, tutoring, or even talking with your siblings.

What qualities should a young writer writing children's novels possess?

- A natural ability to understand how children think, feel, and act in certain situations.
- The ability to write stories from a child's point-of-view.
- An understanding that younger children have a different vocabulary. For example, a child, age eight, rarely talks about a tax budget. He is concerned, though, about how much the candy at the corner is going to cost and if he has enough money.
- Knowing what children fear. For example, the first jump off a diving board or being submerged in water.

If you wish to write for children, get yourself into contact with them and find out what they are really like. Never be afraid to try your ideas out on them; seeing their initial reaction can aid you greatly.

"Growing Up with Different Genres"

by John Greig

The biggest challenge that young writers face is change. Writers need to identify the changes in their writing and decide if these changes are positive or negative. I have identified three changes in attitude in my development as a writer.

When I first began writing seriously at the age of eleven, I was in what I call the "Me" stage. I wrote to please myself. I was bored with the books I could find in my elementary school library. I needed an outlet for my overactive imagination. I really had little desire for others to read my writing and publishing rarely entered my mind.

The next stage of my writing I call the "Who Knows?" stage. "Who Knows?" lasted through my early teenage years. My ideas were changing so rapidly that I never completed my stories—if I wrote at all. My style imitated the style of the author whose book I was reading at the time.

About this age the opposite sex made an entrance. Friends tried to turn me against writing. Writers don't have as much time to themselves because of a part-time job or an increasing social life. Suddenly, romances weren't so "icky."

Life can suddenly become very confusing. I dealt with my confusion by writing poor fantasy. The fantasy I wrote during this time contained static, angelic heroes and wimpy villains. My fantasy worlds were "perfect," because I didn't want to face the problems of my real world. My writing lacked reality. Realism is the secret ingredient of good fantasy.

At age eighteen, I am in the "Me, You, and the Rest of The World" stage. I write shorter stories that satisfy me, and that are strong enough to be accepted by my friends and fellow writers. Hopefully, my stories will be published so the rest of the world can learn from my experiences. My writing is about real topics that people care about.

When a young writer wants to write differently, do it. It is the writer's sense trying to develop a style. Recognize changes in your writing and analyze those changes. The result will be a more complete writer with an individual style.

Learning about Genres

Most young writers I meet are in one of two places regarding learning about genres. The first place I usually find them is that they have been introduced to short stories and poems at school, but they have never seriously looked at what they would love to write. Yet a natural part of growing up is trying out activities related to something we enjoy. For example, if you enjoy running, you will usually try out all different types of running—cross-country, hurdles, 220-yard dash, and maybe even a marathon—to see what you do best. Or you may enjoy singing, in which case you will try singing jazz, musicals, folk, rock, or opera to see what you are best at.

There is no reason in the world not to be writing your own romance novel if that is what you would love to do. Young writers are so used to doing writing because it is asked of them at school. It is an important switch to look at what your interests and background are and how that could give you some clues as to what you indeed write best.

The second place I have found young writers to be in learning genres is that they have found the genre they really love to write but they have never really dug around and found out what the techniques and rules are governing that genre. For example, it is a rare case when I meet a young writer interested in writing children's picture books who knows that picture books are usually a set number of pages. Or the young poet whose images need to be clearer in her poetry, but she has never read any poetry outside what she has been handed in school. Or the young adult mystery novelist who knows her plot is weak, but has never thought of picking up professional writers' reference books on developing plots in mysteries.

KNOW WHERE YOUR WRITING COMES FROM

The selection of a theme is never an accident with any writer; its provenance, however, does sometimes seem to be thrown in one's way like a coin in the sand, which catches the light when one walks past at a certain angle.

Mary Renault

Many unexpected things can start a seed for a writing idea. Here are five areas you can look at to see if they inspire your writing.

Your Favorite Projects

This category is not limited to projects you did at school. You may have done a community project with a group you belong to. You may have done a project with your family. You may have done something entirely by yourself as a hobby.

These projects could indicate your interest in a particular type of writing. For example, I'll never forget the shock I had one day when I realized my first book (a series of mini-biographies of famous Canadians) was almost an exact replica of a school project I did in elementary school on famous people.

You may find that you always enjoyed writing poetry, but had trouble with short story assignments. Or you may have loved writing a history project because it was about a period of time that fascinated you. Your interest in that period could be turned into research for a historical novel or even a thriller with flashbacks to that period in time.

Your Favorite Books

A survey of your favorite authors can uncover the genres you prefer to write in. For example, if J.R.R. Tolkien was on your list, you may have a natural interest in writing fantasy. If you have an appreciation of Alice Munro or O. Henry, you may have an interest in short stories. An interest in Margaret Laurence, Albert Camus, and Pat Conroy may indicate an interest in full-length novels.

Some of the books you read may be simply to escape. A number of people find mysteries the most wonderful books to relax with! Other books may be a reading challenge.

Your Interests

Your interests can indicate your own writing angle or the particular audience you intend to write for. For example, if you have a strong interest in science, you may write science fiction or even science textbooks one day. If you work with young children, perhaps teaching swimming, you may find you have a natural ability to tell stories and hold the interest of children. The hero in your story may be a swimming instructor! If you have an interest in law and plan to become a lawyer, you may end up writing a thriller in your spare time.

Your Writing Skills

Do your writing skills show a tendency for you to write pieces of a particular length? For example, if you are already writing long stories (100 pages or more), you may be a natural candidate for writing novels. Or how about your school assignments? Do you get so involved in the complexities of a history essay that you write twice the word limit? You may be a natural nonfiction book or article writer.

Your Family and Community

Just like some people get handed down the family business, you may find your family and the community you live in a surprising link to your writing. For example, your great grandfather may tell you stories about the war, which you can turn into the background of a short story. Or your father may love electronics, and you turn your ideas about electronics into a children's book.

The point is, outside influences can have a great effect on your writing. If you let your everyday activities, natural interests, and surrounding situations guide you, your writing can only improve for it.

Choose a subject, ye who write, suited to your strength.

Horace, Ars Poetica, *1:38*

ALL SUBJECTS TEACH IMPORTANT SKILLS

If some days you can't seem to sit still during your history or geography class because for some reason what you are learning doesn't seem relevant, try to remember that there are ways to turn some of the material you are learning into useful writing material. Other subjects besides English can enhance your writing/observing/reading ability in fiction and nonfiction writing. For example:

Science —
- teaches observation skills that tie into description.
- applies to science fiction writing.
- applies to nonfiction articles.
- gives information that can be applied to an informational or a conceptual picture book.

History—
- provides facts for settings.
- provides ideas for atmosphere.
- provides ideas for characters' problems related to society.
- can tie nicely into historical fiction projects.

Math—
- is excellent training in problem-solving skills.
- trains student to look for patterns or formulas (extremely useful in nonfiction).
- ties into science fiction/fantasy projects.

Geography—
- gives facts regarding climate and weather patterns for a story.
- gives locations for settings.
- teaches appreciation for the environment.
- can tie into environment projects, song-writing, articles, etc.

Music and Visual Arts—
- teach appreciation of different art forms.
- are excellent training for the senses (audio and visual).
- are outlets for the imagination.
- provide information on what a character may be listening to or even a painting she may have in her house.

STUDYING THE ART FORM

I've seen a new understanding of the art form behind the genre help young writers make important leaps in their writing. Young writers with an interest in writing for children can choose the length and the contents of their books depending on the age group they have decided to work in. Short story writers wishing to move on to writing young adult novels can go from writing three chapters and stopping, to writing ten to fifteen well-structured chapters.

You might think that understanding how picture books developed or understanding why publishers require children's stories to fall into particular age groups will restrict your imagination. Perhaps you believe it will make you feel as if you are following the same tightrope that other writers have walked, when you want to be different from them. But in fact, experience has shown that young writers who are clear on the rules and background behind genres are much more confident about their writing and produce writing of a higher quality.

WRITING FOR AN AUDIENCE

Ask most students who the audience of their writing projects is and they will answer—the teacher. Yet, in real life, the only writer who writes specifically for the teacher audience is the educational writer. The percentage of these writers in the entire population is less than .003%.

You want to shift to thinking in terms of: whom I am really talking to when I write this piece? Am I writing for a particular age group? For example, is it for the general adult public? Is it for children?

After you have answered these questions, the next question applies more to nonfiction writers. Am I writing for a particular age that shares something in common? Is it for sports car owners? Is it for other tennis players?

Authors, magazine writers, and people employed in jobs in which they need to write all write for specific audiences. Audiences consist of everything from sports car drivers, single women, people who own pets, and people who are on diets to people concerned about the environment, scientists, and so on.

You now have the answer to your question of why creative writing assignments handed in to the teacher perhaps don't contain any magic. You may have fallen into the trap of writing a piece for the teacher rather than for a specific audience.

By allowing yourself to think and write for a specific audience, your writing will take on a new focus. Writing for an audience — a known and respected audience — is an important shift that will add relevance to the writing project.

TWO OVERLOOKED GENRES

Nonfiction

If you write excellent school projects and you enjoy writing them, you may be a likely candidate for nonfiction writing. Nonfiction includes magazine articles, how-to books, biographies, information picture books, and many, many more. You may be surprised to find you actually care about nonfiction books. You may also be surprised to find out how much imagination and creativity can go into them.

You can bring all your imaginative powers to your nonfiction. Do this not to change the facts, but to discover unusual angles or fascinating information. Knowing your subject inside out, being able to put your hands on interesting facts, and writing concisely are the prerequisites of excellent nonfiction writing.

Children's Books

Children's books are another area young writers typically overlook, despite the fact that there are stories happening around you all the time when you live in a family.

Children's books have specific page lengths as well as specific age groups. Children's picture books are typically 24, 32, 48, or 64 pages long. Children's nonfiction books are usually 32, 48, 96, 148, or 164 pages long. If you are good at math, you will have realized that all books are a multiple of the number 4. This has to do with the way sheets of paper come off the printing press and how books are eventually made.

ACTIVITIES

The Wide World of Genres

FICTION

Here are some of the genres you can write about if you are interested in writing fiction.

Short Story and Novel	Literary Mystery Adventure Suspense Horror Romance Humor Historical Fiction Science Fiction Fantasy
Poetry Plays	

If you have an interest in writing for children and young adults, be aware that there are five different age groups that the publishing industry produces books for. They are ages: three to five, six to nine, eight to twelve, ten to fourteen, and twelve and up (young adult).

NONFICTION

Here are some of the subjects you can write about if you are interested in nonfiction.

Books Articles Essays Textbooks Professional Reference Books	Biographies Business Environment Science Sports Health Finances Cookbooks

If you are interested in writing for children, you can also write books and articles. Nonfiction picture books are called: information picture books and concept picture books. The five age groups still apply to this market.

Shown is a chart of some of the many different genres in the publishing world. Read the list carefully and think about what genres you write in now. Consider which you might like to try in the future. Choose your three favorite genres that you normally write in. Why are these your favorite? What do you know about their structure?

If you like, use the list and your notebook to record the answers you came up with above. Refer back to your answers every so often during your writing to see if your goals or preferences are changing.

Where Does Your Writing Come From?

As was discussed earlier in this chapter, your writing can have its origins in many different things around you. The questions below can help identify some of your interests and talents that can reveal ideas for your writing.

- What are two projects (at school, in a club, or at home) that you enjoy doing the most?
- Who are your favorite authors?
- What are your main interests?
- What are your best writing skills? (Take these from the previous work on skills.)
- What fields or occupations have your relatives been employed in?

Using your notebook, write at least two answers in response to each of the above questions. Now think about what you have written down. Are there some clues that suggest perhaps you have an interest in a type of writing you didn't really think you had? Come up with two or three genres you think you may now be attracted to.

An Expert in Your Own Genre

There are two types of reading you can do to develop confidence in the genres you are writing in. One, read all the good books in the genre you are interested in. This gives you an invaluable background. If you are interested in writing young adult adventure, read the books that are classics and/or have won awards or prizes in that area.

Two, read some of the how-to books and critical essays

about your chosen genre. Develop a sense of the rules that can and can't be broken.

I call this step in a young writer's development becoming a "reading expert." It is fundamental step for any writer, young or old, who wishes to get published.

The following is a short list of recommended books. They are lots of fun to read and to work through, especially since you can work through them at your own pace.

Where applicable, I have also listed some of the young authors who have been published by major publishing houses. Their listings are noted by a △ symbol.

Fiction—Novel and Short Story

Conrad, Barnaby. *The Complete Guide to Writing Fiction*. Cincinnati: Writer's Digest Books, 1989.

Stanley, G.F. *How to Write Short Stories for Young People*. Cincinnati: Writer's Digest Books, 1986.
Discusses different types of short stories.

Whitney, Phyllis. *Guide to Fiction Writing*. Boston: The Writer, 1982.

Wyndham, Lee. *Writing for Children and Teenagers, 3rd edition*. Cincinnati: Writer's Digest Books, 1988.

Young Adult Novel

△ Behrens, Michael. *At the Edge*. New York: Avon, 1988.

△ Hindle, Lee J. *Dragon Fall*. New York: Avon, 1984.

△ Hinton, S.E. *The Outsiders*. New York: Dell, 1967.

Irwin, Hadley and Eyerly, Jeannette. *Writing Young Adult Novels*. Cincinnati: Writer's Digest Books, 1987.

△ Korman, Gordon. *This Can't Be Happening at MacDonald Hall*. Toronto: Scholastic, 1977.

△ Luiken, Nicole. *Unlocking the Doors*. Toronto: Scholastic, 1988.

△ Putnam, David Binney. *David Goes Voyaging*. New York: G.P. Putnam's Sons, 1925.

Poetry

△ Nolan, Christopher. *Dam-burst of Dreams*. Athens: Ohio University Press, 1988.

Swede, George, Editor. *The Universe is One Poem: Four Poets Talk about Poetry*. Toronto: Simon & Pierre, 1990. (Available from Bookslinger, 2402 University Avenue W., St. Paul, MN 55104 and from Inland Book Co. Inc., P.O. Box 120261, East Haven, CT 06512.)

Children's Picture Books

Brookes, Mona. *Drawing with Children*. Los Angeles: Jeremy P. Tarcher, Inc., 1986.
To all those writers whose drawings consist of stick men, the good news is there is hope. Here is a relatively simple method for dramatically improving anyone's drawing ability.

△ Chbosky, Stacy. *Who Owns the Sun?* Kansas City: Landmark Editions, Inc., 1988.

Hearn, Emily and Thurman, Mark. *Draw and Write Your Own Picture Book*. Richmond Hill: Pembroke, 1989.
Specifically written for the young writer, it is very easy to read (thirty-two pages) and work with.

△ Miller, Jayna. *Too Much Trick or Treat*. Kansas City: Landmark Editions, Inc., 1991.

Roberts, Ellen E.M. *The Children's Picture Book. How to Write It and How to Sell It*. Cincinnati: Writer's Digest Books, 1981.
Discusses three different types of picture books (fiction, information, and concept). It also gives ideas about the differences in writing for the five different age groups.

Horror, Fantasy, and Science Fiction

Editors of *Analog*. *Writing Science Fiction and Fantasy*. New York: St. Martin's Press, 1991.

King, Stephen. *Danse Macabre*. New York: Everest House, 1981.
Traces the development of the horror genre from 1930 to 1980.

Williamson, J.N. *How To Write Horror, Fantasy, and Science Fiction*. Cincinnati: Writer's Digest Books, 1987.

Nonfiction

Roberts, Ellen E.M. *Nonfiction for Children: How to Write It— How to Sell It*. Cincinnati: Writer's Digest Books, 1986.

For books on other types of genres — mystery, romance, comedy, etc.—write to Writer's Digest Book Club, 1507 Dana

Avenue, Cincinnati, OH 45207 to ask for a catalog of their latest books plus information on joining their book club. Also, check your public or school library.

Writing What You Write Best

This is an activity that will take some time and determination on your part, but the rewards you will reap from it will be tremendous. Remember all those questions about "What do I do know"? This exercise will help you answer most of those questions.

This activity is broken into two phases. The first phase is for those young writers who have not really had a chance to explore other genres. The second phase is for those who already know which genre they love and want to know more about the inherent rules and structures. Select the group that best fits where you are at the moment with respect to exploring genres.

Phase One. You may have been selecting genres such as short stories or poetry simply because you have been asked to write these for school. It is time to take a look around and explore what it really takes to write different genres.

Phase Two. You have already explored other genres and have a pretty good idea what genre(s) you prefer to write, but you are not really knowledgeable about how the genre came about and some of its inherent rules. For example, you have written a children's picture book, but don't know what age group it really fits. Or you have written a play, but don't feel it is your best work.

Phase One

If you are in the first group, follow this plan to explore genres. Adapt the plan to suit your own needs where it is necessary. Determine the three different genres you are interested in. Write these in your notebook.

Step 1. For the genres that interest you the most right now, select a book from the recommended reading list in "An Expert in Your Own Genre."

Step 2. Read at least one book that has won an award in that genre. (Your librarian can help you find them.)

You can do Step #1 and #2 for each of the three genres you are interested in, moving at your own pace. Record your steps as you take them, perhaps along with a few notes on ideas and results from your reading. Then, when you are ready, you can move on to Phase Two.

Phase Two

If you are in the second group, or after you complete Phase One, follow this plan. Write down in your activities notebook one or two genres you will *focus* on.

Step 1. Read in-depth one or more books on structure.

Step 2. Read at least three books, preferably by different authors and, if possible, of different nationalities.

Peter's Plan

Three genres I am interested in:
1. Adult Novels
2. Young Adult Novels
3. Mystery Short Stories for Children

Step #1: I will read the chapters I find interesting in one book on structure for each genre:
1. Guide to Fiction Writing
2. Writing for Children and Teenagers
3. How to Write Short Stories for Young People

Step #2: I will read one award-winning book for each genre:
1. Ask librarian about winner of Booker Prize.
2. Dragon Fall
3. Ask librarian about mystery award winners.

Take all the time you need to complete these two phases. They may take you two weeks; they may take you six months, depending on your schedule. Once again, record your steps as you progress, along with comments on your work.

Working on one or two genres with the understanding of how it really works, rather than dabbling all over the place with no clear idea of any genre, helps you to build your confidence. Remember Cinderella, who just naturally slipped into that slipper? Well, that is the sort of fit you want. Somewhere along the line writers have made a decision about what genres they want to work in. It could be for a particular book, for a year, or for the rest of their lives. Then, they sat down and started to write.

Christine's Plan.
Phase Two.

Genres I will focus on:
1. Children's picture books (ages 6-9)
2. Children's novels (ages 8-12)
Step #1: I will read in-depth one or more books on structure:
1. The Children's Picture Book
2. Writing for Children and Teenagers
Step #2: I will read at least 3 books:
Children's picture books (ages 6-9)
1. The Paperbag Princess, by Bob Munsch
2. Madeline, by Ludwig Bemelmans
3. The Snowy Day, by Ezra Jack Keats
Children's Novels (ages 8-12)
1. Mama's Going to Buy You a Mockingbird, by Jean Little
2. The Jungle Book, by Rudyard Kipling
3. Matilda, by Roald Dahl

Research for Fiction and Nonfiction

This activity is for young writers who want to try their hand at either creating a mini-biography (1,500 words) or a historical short story (2,000 words). For the young writer interested in being published, either of these could be used in an educational anthology.

This activity allows you to focus in on a particular day in a famous person's life and create a setting and mood based on information from new sources of research. You will develop skills in researching for unusual facts, building your imagination, developing scenes for different times in history, as well as learning to improve your settings, mood, and atmosphere.

Writing interesting biographies and historical fiction is a combination of finding interesting facts and being capable of placing yourself in a particular period of time.

Where do you go to find really interesting facts? Here are some suggestions.

Unusual dictionaries reveal peculiar language. For example, try *The Dictionary of American Slang* and *The New Grove Dictionary of Music and Musicians*.

Books on a country's customs give you information about national holidays, ethnic festivals, games, festival foods, why certain holidays occur, how a certain holiday is celebrated, and how the people might celebrate New Year's Eve. If you would like to do more on special days and how they might apply to a person chosen for this project, I recommend Carolyn Parry's, *Let's Celebrate* (Toronto: Kids Can Press, 1987). Plus there is *The American Book of Days*, by Jane M. Hatch (New York: H.W. Wilson Co, 1978).

A history book may answer questions such as what people were wearing, what they were eating, the type of newspapers or books they were reading, and what unusual community laws were in place. While researching my book *Madeleine de Vercheres* I came across a whole set of city laws. In the early 1700s in the city of Montreal, one law stated that if you owned a dog it needed to be in the house by 9:00 p.m. That fact alone could be the basis of an interesting children's story!

A geography book may reveal a favorite place a person liked to visit, the climate at a particular time of year, or the surroundings about a person's house.

Letters, journals, or diaries people wrote may show personal thoughts regarding people in their lifetimes, what their homes looked like, and favorite pets.

When I was doing research for a short biography of Lucy Maud Montgomery, her journals proved to be a wonderful source of material regarding childhood superstitions and special occasions at school. One superstition was that if you count nine stars for nine nights, the first boy you shake hands with would be your future husband!

Authors of biography and historical fiction bring their own individual angle to a subject. No two biographies or pieces of historical fiction are the same because of this.

You want to leave your subject's individual imprint. For example, you may choose to: write more about the famous person's family; write about the thoughts the person was having as he created his invention; or focus on the problems he had to overcome as a child or teenager.

Step 1. Choose a famous person to write about.

Step 2. Pick one day in that person's life to write about. It can be any day: a birth, a birthday, the day he invented something, the day before he invented something, the day he died, meeting a special friend, the first day of school, or an event that scared him.

Step 3. There are many questions you can answer in your writing. If there was anything to read—newspaper, books, etc. —what would this person have been reading that day? What type of music would he perhaps have listened to? If he went to work, how would he have gotten there? What clothes would he have put on? If he went to school, what would the school have looked like? What would make this person happy or sad that day? What were his family like? Did he have a close relationship with anyone in particular? Did he have a pet?

Step 4. Using your research, write either a mini-biography of 1,500 words or a 2,000 word short story.

Step 5. Swap your mini-biography or short story with a friend.

Step 6. If you really like your piece, why not try and get it published!

As an option, if you wrote a mini-biography, why not try writing a short story from the same research? You may learn something interesting about the connection between fiction and nonfiction.

Children's Books: Understanding Different Age Groups

This activity allows the young writer interested in writing either fiction or nonfiction children's books to learn about the differences in age groups. You will develop skills in understanding one particular age group in children's literature and creating your own projects. The result will be a nonfiction or fiction book in the subject of your interest.

For children's writers, there are five different age categories you can choose to write in. (If you need to remind yourself, go to the genre chart.)

Step 1. Decide what subject you would like to write about.

Step 2. Decide what age group you would like to write for.

Step 3. Go to the library and find one or two books for that age group. Now find one or two examples in another age group on any subject. (The children's librarian is a good person to help you.)

Step 4. Make two columns on a page in your notebook. Put the name of the book (plus the author) and the age group at the top of each column. Write down what you think makes the age groups different.

Here are some hints. Ages six to nine frequently have: up to 200 words, 6" x 9" book format, simple illustrations, three or four sentences per picture and per page, and small chapters. Ages eight to twelve frequently have: fun, interesting, and bizarre facts, storytelling touch, illustrations, drawings, and photographs slightly more sophisticated and realistic, more up-to-date research, and an interesting, original angle.

Step 5. Gather together the research you need for the subject you have chosen.

Step 6. Decide what angle you will take.

Step 7. Construct two twelve page storyboards like the sample. With the first copy, think of each page and each double-page spread as a camera shot. The reader needs to be able to see the text and the pictures. The more pleasing to the eye, the better the reader will be able to enjoy her book! This is only a rough sketch. Ideas for chapters, titles of chapters, and diagrams and photos need take only a short while.

Here are some hints for the nonfiction board.

- Only the title of the chapters or a simple key word phrase needs to be placed on the pages of the board.
- Chapters can be of the same length to start.
- Illustrations can be represented by squares with a brief word inside them describing the picture or diagram.
- Allow for an introduction.

Step 8. Writing. Take the second storyboard. It's now time to write the text! You can either write small enough to fit into the blanks, or—a better idea—use separate sheets of paper, but put the number of the storyboard page at the top to correspond with your storyboard layout.

These are the typical steps fiction and nonfiction writers go through—organization, design, and selection of material.

Step 9. The next step is putting in the illustrations, then binding the book together with a proper cover and title page.

Presto! You have made a children's picture book!

A further option can be to turn a good school project into a good book. Take a project you have really enjoyed working on. Look at it from the eyes of a five year old. What would make it interesting? Look at it from the eyes of a ten year old. What angle or slant could you use to make it interesting? Look at it from the eyes of a fourteen year old. What style would it have to be written in to make it interesting?

Take the idea that you liked the best from the above three groups. Go to the library and take out three award-winning nonfiction books that are related to your subject (i.e., biography, science, health, etc.).

Using a storyboard, see if you can come up with an idea for a book. (Use the following page lengths. If it was a five year old, twenty-four pages; ten year old, forty-eight pages; fourteen year old, sixty-four pages.) Plot out the chapters. Don't forget that a fair amount of the book will be illustrations.

What did you learn about what it takes to write a good school project and a good nonfiction book? Can you use a lighter, funnier tone? You can do all sorts of neat sidebars and illustrations, rather than formal and stuffy maps and charts. You can let your imagination soar and see what will tempt all different ages of people to read your book.

Chapter 4

Playing with Your Imagination

When you walk down the street, when you sit in school, and when you see a movie, you are making up your mind as to what you like and what you don't like. What you find pleasing to look at or to do reflects your tastes and your viewpoint. Bring your own tastes and viewpoints to your stories, poems, or articles.

Have you ever stopped to think why people are attracted to different things? Why your mother may think looking at the sunset beats seeing any movie? Why your brother loves photography, but you prefer writing?

Young writers put their own signature on the words they choose and the way they arrange them. There is a great similarity between writers and people who catch butterflies. As a writer, you are out in the field of life catching people's imaginations with your words.

Give yourself the time to let your imagination soar.

KEEPING TRACK OF IDEAS

A Favorite Passages File Folder

Often times you may be reading and find yourself saying, "Gee, that was a really great piece of writing." You then flip the page and keep going. Next time, why not mark the page with a Post-it™ or paper-clip, then jot the passage down later into a "favorite passages file folder." The passages that you write down may strike a particular chord one day when you need inspiration for a writing project. Watch for spectacular settings, vivid character descriptions, first encounters, or anything that really catches your imagination.

Here are two of my favorites.

An exquisite scene of a boy trying to get close to his first girlfriend, written by John Fowles in *Daniel Martin*, goes on for pages. It ends with these lines:

"She just stopped and turned, so abruptly that he almost bumped into her; put her hands and the flowers behind her back and simply stared at him, the old game of staring. Five seconds it lasted. Then she closed her eyes and raised her mouth to be kissed. He hesitated, he poised, he somehow found his hands gingerly on her upper arms; then the entire world, or sixteen years of it, melted."

And Gustav Flaubert immortalizes a sound in *Madame Bovary*:

"The stones striking the wooden coffin made that awesome sound which seems to us the reverberation of eternity."

Diaries

Most writers keep a personal diary or journal. How can these help your writing? It really is up to you and the type of records you keep. On one hand, the practice keeps your observational powers sharp. On the other hand, you may have an ongoing question about a problem or person, the recording of which will turn out to be very useful for the basis of a scene in a story. With a very long-term view, you can always use your teenage diaries as research for when you are an adult and looking to write a young adult novel!

Personal diaries are a wonderful way to keep track of your ideas and views. I still have the diaries I wrote as a teenager. I only wish I had kept slightly more interesting ones. A lot of what I thought is carefully kept in cryptic messages about people in my class and my family.

In fact, I seemed to be in a funny diary mode of recording all the NHL hockey games and my tennis scores. Consider the following example from one of my old diaries.

Image Journals

Another type of journal you can use to record ideas for

your writing projects is an "image journal." An image journal is made up of both writing and illustrations. The illustrations can range from photographs you have taken to clippings cut from magazines, postcards, cartoons, etc.

The writing can be your own writing, quotations, and words or paragraphs from an article. An image journal is a fun way to record ideas and images that interest you and that you can later use for your own writing. Perhaps one of the best known images to start off a novel is a photo of a red-haired girl that inspired L.M. Montgomery to write *Anne of Green Gables.*

Thursday March 16

Baked some brownies, mailed my letter to Maarit, & shopped a bit for Mom. Read "The Guns of Navarone." Played tennis with Tom, Sue, & Ian. Court 2 was flooded. Stayed down there until 10:30 with Mom and Mrs. McClelland. Phoned Sandy from club. Dutchess finally came out from under the deck.

Use any blank or lined book you like. You can buy any of these at a stationery store. It is best to use a book that is at least 8½" x 11" since this will give you room for large pictures. You can also use a loose-leaf binder so that you can insert pages and move them around as you please. You may even find that index cards make a good mount for pictures.

Under each image write something about the image. Why do you like it? What appeals to you? Does it remind you of something? Is there a story or poem behind it?

You can keep an image journal for a fantasy, a mystery, or any type of story. For example, you might want to collect pictures of all sorts of unusual characters from comics and magazines to give you ideas for characters in your fantasy stories. Another example is cutting photos out of magazines for scenes in a mystery. You get the idea?

It's also fun to collect images from a particular focus. This is good if you live in a country where there is not a particular type of animal or plant. If you collect close-ups, it's almost as good as being there!

A Special Journal

You can keep any type of journal depending on your writing interests. My girlfriend, Catriona, was working on her first novel and wanted to make sure she was accurately recording the seasons in England. She found it useful to keep a weather diary in which she recorded everything from the first spring flowers to the patterns of thunderstorms. She found using a small desk diary useful.

For example:

June 1. *Another scorching summer day to begin June. Phillip actually got his first case of sunburn. Peonies out. Also some small blue-and-yellow irises. Horse chestnuts in flower: notice variety of color.*

MAKING TIME TO WRITE

Professional writers have a regular writing schedule. Or they have learned to discipline themselves to sit down and write when they need to get a piece finished. The only way to learn what works for you in your writing life is to make the time to write. The more you write, the more you will see of your own writing style. Thoughts you didn't even know you had will take shape on the paper or computer screen. Character sketches will turn into full-dimensional characters with hair, eyes, teeth, personality, and dozens of other interesting things.

If you want to write well, you need to put time aside to learn the craft. It helps to schedule a regular time because you will be setting up important discipline for later on in life. That is, you will train yourself to sit down and write whether you need to or want to.

If you need help releasing yourself from endless hours of school work (and to prepare wisely if you are going to college), you may want to read *Use Your Head*, which is listed at the end of this chapter.

Your regular writing time can be as long or short as you want, depending on your writing aspirations.

When You Write Best

When I am . . . completely myself, entirely alone . . . or during the night when I cannot sleep, it is on such occasions that my ideas flow best and most abundantly. Whence and how these come I know not nor can I force them . . .

Mozart

There are probably more views about when to write than on any other topic in writing. Some people write only when they feel like it; others can't afford to be so free and easy, so they sort out a regular routine.

Try out different parts of the day until you find your best time. Also, think about where you are when you come up with some of your best ideas. I've often been caught on the stairs with the brilliant flash of a whole outline of a book and had to sit down and write it right there on the steps.

ACTUAL CASE STUDIES AT A YOUNG WRITERS' CLUB

Dave found he got inspired by an idea, then his interest would drop off. His excuse for stopping: "I lost interest in the plot."

The solution: After some discussion, Dave started to look at what exactly he was trying to write. Once he had decided it was a short story, rather than just some free form with no direction, he structured a plot outline and found he could finish his original idea.

Shane suffered from "a midnight cowboy" effect. Some nights he could write; others he just couldn't seem to control the idea flow. His excuse for stopping: "No inspiration."

The solution: The whole idea of writing even when he was supposedly "uninspired" was new to Shane. He put a certain amount of time aside every week, and began to write no matter what he felt like. In fact, he commented later that it was a little like getting into homework. Once he was into it, he was fine. But sitting down and getting to work sometimes took more effort.

Sharon started off writing great guns. She wrote for five days in a row, 800 to 900 words on the average. Then she slipped to 200 words. Then she stopped. Her excuse for stopping: "Ran out of time."

The solution: Sharon was in the eighth grade and unused to scheduling for an activity longer than a week. She got a year's calendar and started to schedule her writing for one complete school term. Sharon had been used to attending squash lessons once a week but this was scheduled by her parents. It was a new idea for her to schedule her writing hobby herself.

It is an unpleasant effort to sit down and write; but I find not sitting down and writing even more unpleasant.

William Golding

In each case, the young writer made a commitment to write, ran into an obstacle, and then came up with a solution. Some obstacles were caused by simply having to fit something new into an already busy homework and social schedule. Others were caused by plotting problems, a lack of clarity regarding the genre, or a poorly defined character.

DIVIDE AND CONQUER

It helps when you are planning to do any writing piece to have an idea of the number of pages it will be and how long you want the writing to take you.

Unless you have entered contests in which there is a specific word count, the notion of thinking how many pages your piece will be may be totally foreign to you. Yet if you ask any author working on a current writing project, he can most likely tell you how long his book will be—within fifty pages or so. This is something that comes with practice. But it is also a valuable tool in training you to see the finished book or short story. For those of you who never seem to finish a short story or novel, this might be an interesting thought to consider.

One year in my private consulting, I had the pleasure of working with a boy who had always wanted to write a horror novel. Previously, he had only written short stories. They were usually ten pages long (2,500 words). He wrote them when he felt like it.

Under my guidance, he decided to try writing a hundred page novel. The whole notion of scheduling was new to him, so we worked out a schedule together. To sort out his schedule he did the following calculations:

First, he figured out how many words there were to a type-written double-spaced page. He came up with 250 words (which is fairly standard).

Second, he multiplied 100 pages x 250 words a page. He found that meant he would be writing 25,000 words.

Three, he looked at how long it had taken him in the past to write one short story of 2,500 words. He figured it took about one week of writing for a total of five hours. Thus, in one week he could produce ten pages; and in ten weeks he would have his hundred page novel.

Now obviously that didn't include time for detailed character sketches or plot outlines, but Aric could use this as a rough guide.

Finally, he marked off his calendar and assigned a chapter for each week. Then he got to work!

You don't need to use quite the same method that we did. You can adapt it to suit your own needs. But it really helps to set a realistic schedule for getting a writing piece finished.

John Fowles reports writing 10,000 words a day while working on the first draft of *The French Lieutenant's Woman*.

ORGANIZING YOUR WRITING

Outlines

You have most likely learned some type of outline in school—either in answering questions for an English test or in following a simple plot outline for a writing assignment.

In outlining a short story or novel, writers use all sorts of methods. Some use a visual aid (a storyboard), some use a verbal aid (a plot outline or a one paragraph synopsis of the action of the whole book), some use a combination of the two, and some just get a vague outline in their heads.

The point is not to argue about which method is best because obviously all writers have their own method. The point is, what do you do as a young writer when your story has died midstream and you can't seem to resuscitate it?

Storyboards

Using a storyboard as a guide is one wonderful way of organizing your thoughts for fiction or nonfiction writing. It provides a visual outline of where you are going. Storyboards are most commonly used for picture books as a way to draw the story first and then write in the words. Nonfiction writers and novel writers can use them as visual aids.

I use them because I am very concerned with how my nonfiction books are designed. I keep a sense of what each double-page spread looks like in my head so I know the reader can read the book easily and have fun with it. It is not unusual to find one whole wall of my writing room plastered with current chapter outlines and storyboards.

A storyboard can be used for just about any type of writing —picture books all the way through to full-length nonfiction books. You can make your own storyboard by simply drawing the same number of squares as the number of pages in the article, book, or play you are working on. Use blank paper and keep a master copy so you can photocopy it easily rather than making a new storyboard each time round.

WHAT MAKES YOUR WRITING UNIQUE?

A wonderful quote to remember is from Maryanne Kovalski: "I cannot shout loudly enough how important it is to keep one's eyes open. If you long to write or draw well—you must be willing to look, look and look again with great concentration."

A young person leaves her individual mark in her writing in a number of ways, including: dialogue, vocabulary, characters' descriptions, choice of subjects, preference for certain lengths or forms of writing, introductions, endings, how far she challenges herself with a plot, the degree of the character's problem she is willing to tackle, and much more.

Three-Dimensional Characters

Most stories are started because a circumstance that a person may be caught in has caught our imagination. We can see the main characters really well, along with their dilemma and the possible solutions. In almost any type of fiction writing, you want your characters to be remembered by your reader. There has to be something that catches the reader's interest and emotions.

You want your characters to have this sense of realism too.

Remember what it is like to hold a camera up to your eye and then place the subject of your photo within the small box of your camera lens? Beginner photographers are relieved if

> My characters get talked about at the dinner table as if they are real people.
>
> *Judy Blume*

they manage not to cut off a friend's head during the shot or if they manage to avoid the ugly telephone pole in the background. Learning to write fully-developed characters takes imagination and practice.

If you've managed to get the physical descriptions straight, you want to think about what they are really like. Can you hear their voices in your head? Is the voice high or deep? Quick or slow? What accent do they have? Being able to hear the voices may help you to write dialogue.

One way to make your characters more rounded is to know more about them than you need to know for the plot of your story. Imagine you are meeting them for the first time, interviewing them on television. What would you want to ask them? What would you like to know about them?

> I was writing chapter three of *Homecoming* and out of the darkness of the typewriter, she leapt . . . I could hear what she was saying, and begun making notes.
>
> *Cynthia Voigt describing the creation of Grandmother Tillerman in* The Homecoming.

Settings

Do your settings sound like the same interior designer has decorated all your characters' houses and their rooms?

When you are writing settings, close your eyes and pretend you are the character actually seeing that particular setting at that particular time of day in that particular weather. Better yet, if you can, visit the place you are describing—or at least a similar place—to get a sense of the smells, colors, atmosphere, and so on. Take notes and bring them home with you.

Plots

If for some reason your plot has malfunctioned in the middle of your story, try the following *Plot Breakdown Repair Kit.*

Here are some questions to ask yourself if you are having trouble with part of your plot. Answering these questions about your characters should help resolve things and give you the details and reasons your characters need to be real and compelling.

Your Main Character:
1. What is it your main characters are trying to achieve or become?
2. What are their reasons (why is it so important, or vital) for this objective?
3. Have you set up incidents in your story so that their reasons are clear?

The Person(s) or Thing in the Way:
1. Is this person or object clear in your mind?
2. What are the reasons for the person or object being the way they are?
3. Have you set up incidents or structured the dialogue so this is clear?

Setting up the Initial Action and Complications:
1. What do your main characters do to achieve their goals?
2. If this doesn't work, what do they do next?
3. If this doesn't work, what do they do next?

The Crisis Point:
What is the decision your main characters make at the crucial point of having or not having their objective in their grasp?

Convincing the Reader:
Do the above four elements add up to an interesting story that will captivate your readers? If not, you need to go back and fine-tune it. Check which step doesn't seem to work. If it all seems to work well in your head, it's time to write.

REWRITING

The willingness to rewrite and create the best piece possible is a sign of a conscientious writer. Often times, young writers have got one part of their story or article down pat. When I give feedback, I usually try to help young writers focus on one element of their writing that needs work. It is often difficult and time-consuming to see what is wrong with your work and what can improve it.

I was working on the proof of one of my poems all morning, and took out a comma. In the afternoon, I put it back again.

Oscar Wilde (attributed)

For example:

"Kara, you seem to have a really good grip on your dialogue. How about digging into your settings so we can see where your characters live? How long do you think that will take you? By next week? Fine. Will you show it to me then?"

"John, your images are much stronger. Congratulations. What do you think about the plot structure? You lost me at this point in your story. What were you trying to say or have happen? Oh, really? Good. Can you rewrite that then and let me see it tomorrow?"

"Trudi, you want to make this short story into a novel? We'll just be working on short stories this term, but if you would like to explore ways of making it into a novel, why not read a book by Lee Wyndham that actually gives you some tips?"

READING YOUR WORK ALOUD

Another way to get feedback on your writing is by reading your work aloud to others. Here are some tips.

Some people are masters at reading their books, and others seem barely able to get the words out. There is probably

When I read I try to sound like I'm not reading, like I'm instead the old uncle on the back porch bullslinging away.

Lesley Choyce, author of An Avalanche of Ocean

nothing more disappointing to a group of avid readers of your work to come and hear you read from your work only to find out you don't read well. If you have ever attended authors' readings, you know what I am talking about.

If you are interested in reading from your work, stand up straight and speak clearly. Plus, you could join a storytelling group to learn techniques in storytelling, listen to tapes of well-recorded books, and go to authors' readings at your local libraries or cultural arts center. Most important, always take the opportunity to read your work aloud.

In your support group, or with a friend at home or school, ask someone you respect to rate your reading aloud on a scale of one to ten. Get constructive comments about how you can improve. Here are four tips to help you when you read aloud. One, make sure the whole room can hear you. Two, pronounce your words clearly. Three, take a breath once in a while to make sure you aren't speeding through your work. Four, change the tone of your voice for different characters.

In England, Radio 4's "Book at Bedtime" is the most accessible source of hearing books aloud. The books aren't always read by the author. In Toronto, Canada, there are readings all year round at Harbourfront. Books on tape are also very popular today. Some of them are abridged; some are full-length; some are read by the authors; and some are read by professional actors and actresses. Most bookstores carry them, as well as most libraries. Listen to some to pick up tips on reading your work aloud.

THOUGHTS ON MY WRITING

The following was written by Peter Saunders, a young writer sixteen years old.

"I love to describe. This shows in my writing. I love to imagine things and then tell the world about them, on paper. I love to create, both through words and through pictures, although I am much better with words than with pictures, for with words, I can describe things which I could never draw. Although not all of my best work is fiction, my favorite is.

"I do not love to write dialogue. I am always attempting to make good use of this particular element of writing, but my words begin to sound unnatural when they are meant to be spoken. Thus, I am more likely to describe a scene through adjectives than through the speech of the characters.

"I do not pretend to know a lot about writing. At this stage, I am an amateur; nothing more. I do not write enough, but I strive to be published with some regularity. My writing is still quite juvenile; I often rewrite stories I wrote years before, making extensive changes, and sometimes inventing an entirely new plot.

"My writing is getting better. In fact, the improvements are obvious. They are what keep me going. My most recent story is almost always my favorite story in the world ... I love my writing. If I didn't, I wouldn't do it at all."

ACTIVITIES

The following is a list of activities for improving your characters, choice of words, plots, and settings. These activities are for all types of writers: nonfiction writers, poets, and novelists. Why? Nonfiction writers need to be able to visualize accurately the person of a biography (especially if the person is dead). Poets need to be especially sensitive to the play of words. Short story writers and novelists need to learn to avoid the most common complaints of editors: underdeveloped characters and poorly developed stories.

Timesheet

There are two parts to the activity. The first is to see what your current writing habits are. The second part allows you to get a sense of a schedule for a current writing project.

Following are some questions you need to answer to determine your current writing habits.

How much time do you spend writing? One hour a week; one hour a day; two hours a day.

If you have never spent three hours a day writing, why not? You just write, and when you run out of ideas, you stop; you write for an hour, then read a novel; it has honestly never occurred to you.

How much free time a week do you have to write? How many hours do you actually write? What is the ratio? Are you writing as much as you want to a week?

If not, how many hours or how many words do you want to write a week? What would you have to do to make this work? You may find it easier to schedule writing during a summer vacation or winter or spring break.

Now take a look at a writing project you would like to start or are currently working on. Below is a sample of a young writer's approximated project time and word count. Figure out your own estimates based on this sample, and record your calculations in your activities notebook.

Sample

Marlene, age sixteen, recently received the October issue of *Seventeen* and saw the rules for a short story contest. She decides to write a 2,000 word short story for the *Seventeen*

Magazine/Dell Fiction Contest before Christmas. To help her organize her time, she uses the following timetable.

1. The length of the piece = 2,000 words.
   Divided by the number of words on a double-spaced typewritten page (250 words) = 8 pages.
2. The number of hours a week she has to write is 4 hours.
3. The number of weeks she has to spend on the project is 5 weeks.
4. 4 hours every 5 weeks = 20 hours for her to work on her short story.
5. 2,000 words divided by 20 hours = 100 words/hour.

This gives Marlene a realistic idea of how many words she needs to write each hour she sits down to write. Obviously, some days she may do more and some days she may write less, but she has a realistic target. It also helps her when planning her plot outline. She has a good idea of how long each segment of her story needs to be.

You can also use this chart for much longer projects, such as the Avon/Flare Novel Contest, which requires 125 to 250 pages. Or, if you like to write and illustrate your own books, you can plan your drawing and writing time and submit your piece for The Written & Illustrated by . . . Awards Contest run annually by Landmark Editions.

You can also use this method very successfully for school projects!

But remember to modify this timetable to work for you. All writers have their own particular habits and schedules that work for them. Just make sure you are giving yourself enough time to really write the best piece possible — and complete your piece in time to submit it to a contest or publisher.

Marlene's Timetable						
Mon.	**Tues.**	**Wed.**	**Thurs.**	**Fri.**	**Sat.**	**Sun.**
	1	1		1	1	
Total Hours = 4						

Construct a chart outlining the time you want to spend writing each day and each week. Total the hours to see if this is the amount of time you were hoping for. Are you surprised at the amount? Think about your other activities and decide if there is anything you do that is less important to you than your writing. Substitute your writing in this time-frame. You may find that a calendar is an easier way of keeping a schedule of your writing time.

I go up to my study at nine. If I'm working on a new story, I'm usually worn out by 2 p.m.

Paul Jennings, a favorite Australian children's author

What Makes Your Writing Unique?

Listed below are some of the major parts of a writer's style. Honestly rate yourself on how well you incorporate these skills into your writing. As in other exercises, a '3' can stand for good; '2' for adequate; and '1' for undeveloped. As you work on your writing, consider those skills you rated yourself adequate or undeveloped on, and come up with ways you can improve in these areas. Record your answers and solutions in your activities notebook.

- Characters
- Sense of Language
- Plot Setting
- Knowledge of Structure

There are a few other questions you ask yourself to help identify the strengths and weaknesses of your writing. What do you like best about your writing? What do you like least? What would you like to improve?

Mind Stretchers

Write a paragraph or so about the following scenarios in your notebook.

A space creature has arrived in your science classroom. She is only 2" high, but can speak all earth languages, and is sitting right underneath your desk. Get underneath your desk and have a look at the classroom through her eyes. What would your teacher look like? You? Your books? The lights? Any of the unusual objects in your classroom? How would you look to her?

You have woken up one morning to find you are a member of the opposite sex and in a bedroom that clearly belongs to the opposite sex. You shut your eyes hoping all will return to normal once you open them again. You open your eyes. Nothing has changed. You stifle a scream and run to the closet mirror. Describe what you look like. What are your thoughts? What clothes do you decide to put on? What is in your room? Now that you are a member of the opposite sex, what do you think of your parents? Your best friend? Your boyfriend or girlfriend?

Your Own Character Sheet

One of the most common mistakes young writers make is not developing their characters. Your characters may be your strength in your writing; they may be your weakness. Let's see how you measure up!

Take two stories that you have written. Select the one character in each story whom you have described the best or whom you are the most fond of.

One of the tricks to developing a fuller character is to answer questions that arise in the reader's mind about your character. The purpose of this exercise is to see what questions you normally answer when you sit down to write about a character.

Here are some basic physical details to help you get started: name, sex, age, height, skin color, hair color, eye color, and clothes, to name a few.

Did you have any more? Great! But now that you think about it, are there some other details you could have added? How about non-physical details, such as likes, dislikes, or hobbies. Suggestions: school, favorite sayings, something they would be lost without, how other family members perceive this character, what makes your character sad, happy, mad.

Improving Characters and Their Dialogue

If your story has an adult of either your parent's or grandparent's age, try this for a day. Listen carefully to what they say. Do they have favorite words or expressions? Listen to what they really say when you come home from school, when they are trying to encourage you, or when they are telling you to do something differently.

Notice how they stand when they speak. Notice how they sit when they relax. Do they have a favorite object they like to carry around with them? Do you know why or have you ever asked them why?

Now do the same for yourself. What do you say when you are annoyed, happy, confused? Look at yourself in the mirror and write a fully detailed physical description of yourself.

Have you noticed that people don't speak the same way? Good! They use different words and expressions. Avoid another common mistake, and make sure your characters have their own specific dialogue. Recording in your notebook the expressions and habits of people around you can be extremely helpful when you begin to develop a character. Perhaps you can base his actions on those of someone you know!

Your main character may need space. Don't have too many characters fighting for the center stage. Jean Little had to cut down the role of Jeremy's younger sister in *Mama's Going to Buy You A Mockingbird*, because she was detracting from the story.

Improving Settings

Take a story you have written. Take a setting from it. Then think of a place resembling it that you live close to or you have a photo of.

Go to the place that resembles it, or get out the photo. Look at it closely. Can you see anything you may have missed in your description of it? Have you caught the colors, the textures, the smells? Reread what you have written about that setting, and then improve your setting with the added description and details you have picked up from your study.

Reading

Here is a select list of books that can help you with all aspects of your writing:

Brande, Dorothea. *Becoming A Writer*. Los Angeles: Jeremy P.

Tarcher, 1981.
Practical ideas on how to increase the amount of words you write in one sitting, plus how to overcome any "writer's block."

Buzan, Tony. *Use Your Head*. London: Ariel, 1974.
My all-time favorite book on understanding the brain, plus how to study more effectively, read quicker, research sensibly, and develop your own ways of thinking.

McCutcheon, Randal. *Can You Find It?* Free Spirit Press, 1989.
Without doubt the funniest book I've encountered on finding anything. A definite must for young writers looking for unusual research material.

Peck, Robert Newton. *Fiction is Folks*. Cincinnati: Writer's Digest Books, 1983.
Laugh your way to writing better, unforgettable characters.

Roberts, Ellen E.M. *Nonfiction for Children*. Cincinnati: Writer's Digest Books, 1986.
Takes you step by step through the different requirements of each children's age group.

Stanley, George F. *Short Stories For Young People*. Cincinnati: Writer's Digest Books, 1986.
Suggests one way of plotting outlines for short stories.

Wright, John. *The Writing Machine: A Writer's Guide to Creative Computer Use*. Ringwood: Penguin, 1990.

Wyndham, Lee. *Writing for Children and Teenagers*. Cincinnati: Writer's Digest Books, 1988. (3rd edition).
Suggests the synopsis approach. Highly recommended for writers who get stuck in the middle of their stories or want to know how to move from a short story to a novel.

Chapter 5
Learning about the Publishing Industry

Literature is like any other trade; you will never sell anything unless you go to the right shop.
George Bernard Shaw

Have you ever gone shopping and been in such a rush to get a pair of jeans that you've grabbed the first pair that seemed to fit? When you got home, you found they fit okay but not perfectly. Well, that is what seems to happen to novice writers trying to get published.

They are in such a rush to get published, they just send their manuscript off to the first publisher they *think* is right. They wait hopefully. They eventually receive a rejection slip because the publisher doesn't publish that type of story.

What are two stores you often go to that sell the same type of merchandise (clothes, records, jewelry, or whatever)? Great. Who are the designers, the manufacturers, the makers, the recording labels that you buy? Why do you sometimes buy from one type of clothes designer and another time the other? What is it you expect from them?

A publisher is really no different from a car manufacturer, a clothes designer, or a recording company. Each publisher tries to develop a particular look or "list." The publisher will have spent years developing a particular line of books or a particular look to a magazine.

You can't expect to sell your science fiction book to a publisher that specializes in romance. But you would be surprised to know how many novice writers send their writing to the wrong publisher. Somewhere in their careers, the penny drops, and they realize they have to learn the particular image or list of different publishers.

THREE AREAS TO CONSIDER

For young writers there are really three areas of publishing. First, there is mainstream publishing. It is made up of trade publishers, which publish the books you see sold in bookstores. Second, there are educational publishers, who publish the textbooks you use in school and books for teachers and professors. (The best place to learn about these publishers is in reference books that all professional writers use. They are called market guides.)

There is a third area that has recently developed specifically to encourage young writers. These publishers are people who think it is important that young writers' work gains an audience. This "young writers' market" consists primarily of contests run by mainstream publishers (e.g., Avon's novel contest) and magazines that publish young writers' work and run contests. The best source for this "young writers' market" is Kathy Henderson's *Market Guide for Young Writers*.

Market Guides

Most countries have a *Writer's Market* or *Writer's Handbook* listing book and magazine publishers. These books can be 1½ to 2 inches thick. Don't be put off by the sheer size of them. Once you learn how to use one, you will refer to it often. If you can, get a copy of *Market Guide for Young Writers*, which is specifically designed to introduce the young writer to a market guide.

To get the most out of the adult reference market guides, start by looking at the table of contents. Mark the sections that are of interest to you. *The Writer's Market* published by Writer's Digest in the U.S. (the resource book for both Canadian and American writers) has a section called "Using *The Writer's Market*," which gives you some help. *The Writer's Handbook* published by Macmillan/Pen in England has a table of contents from which you can work your way through the book.

FINDING PUBLISHERS

One way of finding publishers is to use *The Writer's Market*, *The Poet's Market*, *The Short Story and Novel Market*, *Market Guide for Young Writers*, or whatever market guide is best suited to your type of writing. At first, try just to read a few entries. Next time through, work out a system of highlighting or marking publishers that hold some interest for you.

Another way to find publishers is to use your own library at home, your local library, or your local bookstore. If you are looking at books in your local library or bookstore, take a pen and pad of paper with you and preferably keep one hand free so you can write. Look for books that are in the genre you prefer to work in. Check who the publishers are.

You will always find the publisher of a particular book on the copyright page. That is the page where you will also find: the author, the year the book was published, and the ISBN number, which is very helpful if you are trying to order the book from a bookstore. It is always a very good idea to be able to know a book by the author's name, the title, and the publisher.

For nonfiction, you will get a good idea of what sort of design and cost of packaging the publishers are committed to by flipping through their books. You will also get a sense of the editor's preferences. Make sure you are looking at current books to make the best judgments here.

A Note for Nonfiction Writers

The mistake unpublished nonfiction writers want to avoid is to think that if a publishing house already has a book on a particular subject, then their book will be competing with it, and therefore they should send it to a publisher that doesn't have a book on that subject at all.

This is exactly opposite of how the publishing game works. You are more likely to get your book published if there are already books selling strongly in an area the publisher is already marketing.

THE PUBLISHER/EDITOR/AUTHOR LINK

Most of the books and magazines that we read today are

Published by Shoe Tree Press, an imprint of
Betterway Publications, Inc.
P.O. Box 219
Crozet, VA 22932
(804) 823-5661

Cover design by Susan Riley
Typography by Park Lane Associates

Copyright © 1990 by Kathy Henderson

Library of Congress Cataloging-in-Publication Data

Henderson, Kathy
    Market guide for young writers / by Kathy Henderson. -- 3rd ed.
      p. cm.
    Includes index.
    Summary: Includes publishing information for the budding writer, including tips on preparing a manuscript for submission, advice from editors, profiles of published young writers, and addresses of publications and contests to which manuscripts may be sent.
    ISBN 1-55870-175-3 : $10.95
     1. Children as authors. 2. Authorship--Handbooks, manuals, etc.
3. Authorship--Competitions. [1. Authorship--Handbooks, manuals, etc. 2. Authorship--Competitions.] I. Title.
PN171.C5H4 1990
808'.02'0835--dc20   90-38770
                                  CIP
                                  AC

Printed in the United States of America
0 9 8 7 6 5 4 3 2

designed, printed, and distributed by someone other than the author. The author is responsible for producing the finest writing possible and earning money in the process. The publishers are committed to keeping their businesses operating (earning a profit) and will usually be interested in a specific type of writing.

A publisher is someone whose business is to design, print, and distribute books, magazines, or related material. An editor is the person in the publishing house who is hired to decide what books will be published and then work with the author in producing the best book. The editor is the person the author will work together with most closely.

The publishing industry is a business. Just as your local candy store can't stay in business if it doesn't sell candy, publishing houses can't stay in business if they can't sell their books. Publishers have to make a profit (bring in more money than they spend) to stay in business.

The books they choose to publish need to sell. As a result,

most publishers have a good idea of what books they can sell. Most book editors will have a certain page length in mind for their books. The same is true for magazine editors. They will usually have a certain word length in mind as to what will work in their magazines.

Submit your work only after you've really looked at the market. Submitting your manuscript and waiting for a reply can take a long time. So you want to make sure you are sending it to the most suitable publisher in the first place. Don't waste your time sending it to the wrong place. Do your research first!

The industry may not make a lot of sense to you at first, but slowly the pieces of the puzzle will start to fall together. In this chapter, you'll be doing some of the steps to collect the first pieces you need to get published successfully. If you do these simple steps now, you will save yourself a tremendous amount of time later, as well as avoid getting unnecessary rejection slips.

SUCCESS STORIES

Concerned with the way people were stereotyping gangs, Susan Hinton, while still attending high school, wrote a forty-page story that grew into the bestseller, *The Outsiders*. Nicole Luiken started to write during her hour-long bus ride to school in Alberta, Canada. In 1988, at the age of seventeen, two of her manuscripts, *Unlocking the Doors* and *Escape to the Overworld*, had been published. In Ireland, school-aged Christopher Nolan, unable to use his limbs or to speak, used a "unicorn stick" fastened to his forehead to hit the keys of a typewriter and penned his first book of poetry, *Dam-burst of Dreams*. In the 1920s, David Binney Putnam at the age of thirteen traveled with his famous publishing father, George Putnam, to the Galapagos Islands. On his return home, he wrote *David Goes Voyaging*, which became the first in a series of books for boys. Gordon Korman wrote *This Can't Be Happening At MacDonald Hall*, his first of a series of young adult novels, as the result of a seventh grade school assignment. In 1987, Stacy Chbosky, at age fourteen, had her first book, *Who Owns the Sun?*, published by Landmark Editions, and it was subsequently made into a movie.

Many novice writers hope to one day be published. As you can see from the examples above, a handful of young writers have managed to be published by major book publishers. An even larger number have been published in special magazines for young writers.

PUBLISHING OPPORTUNITIES IN OTHER COUNTRIES

Remember the phrase "No man is an island"? You may one day be published in another country and/or another language. Why? There may be a larger market for your work in another country.

A larger market means you can sell more books and more people will read your books. This is something any young writer in Canada, Sweden, or Australia may already be aware of since they have neighbors with large populations.

Here are two charts that will give you a better idea of what other countries, some of which may not have occurred to you, may present opportunities because of their populations.

Some Countries and Their Populations
(Figures to the right are the population in millions.)

China	1,119.6
India	831.9
Russia	291.3
United States	248.0
Japan	122.7
Pakistan	113.0
Germany	73.2
Italy	57.4
United Kingdom	55.8
France	55.4
Poland	39.0
Canada	27.1
Australia	16.7
Norway	4.2

**The Most Spoken Languages around the World
(Figures to the right are in millions.)**

Mandarin	844
English	437
Hindi	338
Spanish	331
Russian	291
Arabic	192
Bengali	181
Portuguese	171
Malay-Indonesian	138
Japanese	122
French	119
German	118

A YOUNG AUTHOR'S EXPERIENCE OF BREAKING INTO PUBLISHING

Jennifer Carnell, England

I wrote my first novel, a children's book called "The Return of Count Dracula," when I was thirteen years old. It was submitted to an agent and to numerous British publishers, but unfortunately it received an equal number of rejections. In retrospect, I can see that this was not so very surprising because while I still think that the book was extremely good for my age, it was not a particularly original story and there was too much plot crammed into 180 pages, which made it seem overdone. Sadly, rejection slips seem to be almost inevitable when one is trying to be published, and although it can be very depressing, you should not give up, nor assume that just because one publisher turns you down that another will do the same.

Three years later, I had better luck when I wrote an adult novel entitled "Murder, Mystery and Mayhem," a comic pastiche of the English detective novels of the 1930s, which I hoped would appeal to publishers more than the earlier novel's theme of the dastardly doings of vampires. To my delight, Collins Publishers expressed an interest in the work. They asked me to do some rewriting (to lengthen a rushed ending), after which it was accepted and published by Collins in Great

Britain and Australia, and a year later in the United States by HarperCollins.

The time of publication was very exciting, particularly seeing the front cover, and I was asked to do newspaper, radio, and television interviews, which were both interesting and nerve-wracking. This led onto other things as I was asked to write several articles and review books and I was also eligible to join the Crime Writers Association, which gives me the opportunity to meet other writers. If you do succeed in getting published, do take advice from other people, as publishers run a business and may not always tell you things unless you ask! Lastly, good luck!

CONTESTS AND AWARDS

You may or may not have heard of the major awards for writers who are already published. In Canada, they include the Governor-General Awards and the Mr. Christie Award. In the United States, the Newberry Medals, and Horn Book Awards are coveted prizes. In England, the Mr. Smartie Award and the Booker Prize are well-recognized. Those awards are given to works already published and the publisher in fact submits the manuscript for the award.

Submitting your writing for contests and awards is another way of getting published. This is just a very short list of contests and awards specifically for young people. This list is for unpublished works submitted by the young writer. Write for further information if you are interested in knowing how to enter or qualify.

The Local vs. National Question

Usually school experiences leave us with a sense that one should start off submitting things locally. Then, and only then, if we are any good, do we move up to compete provincially or statewide or nationally. Sending our manuscripts out of the country may feel very unnatural.

Rarely do I find that young writers have a market waiting for them in their own hometown or city. There might be a few publications or contests, but they may not be the right ones for your work. The market for your work may indeed be within the province or state, or even in another country.

Don't be put off by the fact that a contest you enter is on the other side of your country. It may be the perfect place for you to enter. It can also be rather exciting.

Australia

The Kitty Archer-Burton Award

Awarded biennially for verse by a youth under nineteen. For information, write to: Marjorie Wilke, Federal President, Society of Women Writers (Australia), GPO Box 2621, Sydney NSW 2001.

National Book Council/Quantas New Writer's Award

Open to any book of literary merit by a young writer under thirty-five. For information, write to: Executive Secretary, NBC, 1st Floor, 203 Lygon Street, Carlton, Victoria 3053.

Canada

Air Canada Award

Awarded by the Canadian Authors Association to a Canadian writer under the age of thirty deemed to show the most promise for the future in the field of literary creation. For information write to: C.A.A., 104-121 Avenue Road, Toronto, Ontario M5R 2G3 (416) 926-8084.

National Arts Center Playwrights Search

Ages thirteen to nineteen. One- or two-act plays. Must live in southern Ontario or western Quebec. For information, write: Box 1534, Station B, Ottawa, Ontario K1P 5W1.

YTV Achievement Award

Awarded to a promising young writer under nineteen years of age. For information, write to YTV Canada, Inc., YTV Achievement Awards, P.O. Box 1060, Station B, Toronto, Ontario M5T 2T8.

England

Authors' Club First Novel Award

Award for the most promising first novel of the year. Entries for the award are accepted from publishers. For information, write to: The Authors' Club, 40 Dover Street, London, England W1X 3RB

The BBC Wildlife Awards for Nature Writing

Prize for the best essay on nature by a young writer aged thirteen to seventeen. Also a prize for twelve and under age group. For information, write to: Editor, BBC Wildlife Magazine, Broadcasting House, Whiteladies Road, Bristol, England BS8 2LR.

Eric Gregory Trust Fund Awards

Submission of a published or unpublished volume of poetry, drama poems, or belles-lettres. Open to writers under age thirty. For information, write to: Society of Authors, 84 Drayton Gardens, London, England SW10 98B

The *Times*/Jonathan Cape Young Writers Competition

5,000 pounds plus publication for a first work of fiction or nonfiction written in English by an author under the age of thirty. For information, write to: Jonathan Cape, 32 Bedford Square, London, England WC1B 3EL

Unicorn Theater, Young Playwright's Competition

For young playwrights four to six; seven to nine; and ten to twelve. Performance of play after workshop with member of the Theater Club. For information, write to: Unicorn Theater for Children, Arts Theater, Great Newport Street, London, England WC2H 7JB.

United States

A complete listing of contests and awards for young writers can be found in Kathy Henderson's *Market Guide for Young Writers, Third Edition* (Crozet, Virginia: Betterway Publications, Inc., 1990).

BOOK FAIRS

If you live in or near a city where there is an annual book fair for publishers and booksellers (Bologna, Italy; Frankfurt, Germany; London, England; in Canada and the United States the site changes each year), you can most likely attend as a visitor. Sometimes there are free seminars you can attend. Just walking around will give you a good sense of what seems to sell and who sells what.

The London International Book Fair runs in late April. The Bologna Children's Book Fair takes place in early May.

The American Bookseller's Association Convention is in early June, while the Canadian Bookseller's Association Convention is in early July. The Frankfurt Book Fair is held in mid-October.

A HEALTHY ATTITUDE

All writers have their own reasons for submitting their works for publication. The reasons can range from earning money to influencing people's ideas and attitudes. There is no need to feel that you need to get published right now.

Submitting your writing is very personal. It also builds important skills. Skills such as: knowing the audience you are writing for; setting a date as to when your piece of writing is finished; finishing the project on time; preparing the manuscript for submission; typing it up and getting two envelopes ready (one an SASE); and knowledge of the right place to get published. All these skills are relevant to the day-to-day life of being an author.

You may write a nonfiction article on a hobby and have no qualms about submitting it. On the other hand, you may want to submit a short story, but are concerned about whether it is good enough. While these thoughts are only natural, it is useful to keep in mind the question, "What is it that I really want?" and keep focusing on that rather than any self-doubts.

If you don't get published, you may be learning that your writing is not appropriate for the publisher you selected (very important to know), or that you need to work on your writing some more. Perhaps more uncontrollable factors are involved. The publisher's editor turned down the piece because the book won't sell enough copies to make money; they already have a book like that signed for this coming season; the editor doesn't like it personally; the publisher doesn't like it; etc.

If you get published, you are developing confidence in being able to write for a particular market, magazine, or contest. Think of getting an offer to have a piece of writing published as like reaching the top of an iceberg. You may have spent a lot of time swimming around to actually reach it. Upon reaching it, you discover that there is a colossal number of things happening underneath the surface.

All sorts of questions about how the publishing industry works will bob up to the surface. How do books get promoted? How does one become a famous writer? These questions are answered by reading more books and talking to other authors and publishers. Learning about the publishing industry is absolutely essential.

Remember: In the beginning of a book writer's career it is possible that one-third of your time is spent writing, one-third is spent finding a publisher and signing the contract, and the last third is spent in promoting your own books.

✎_____**ACTIVITIES**

Finding the Right Publisher

The purpose of this activity is to teach you the steps all writers have to go through if they would like a piece of writing published. With time, you will build up a working knowledge of which publishers are of interest to you. But in the beginning, you need to do these basic steps. Don't shy away from this exercise; it will teach you all sorts of interesting things.

You'll see your first publisher's catalog. You may even find books of interest that you've never heard of before. (I found a superb book by Peter Dickinson, *Eva*, because it was listed as winning a number of awards on the back pages of the Delacorte Press catalog.)

You need one of your own writing pieces to make this exercise work, preferably one you would like to get published eventually, or a piece in the same genre as what you would eventually like to get published in. If it doesn't have a title, give it a working (temporary) title.

The example given illustrates the steps you will need to follow in determining what publishing houses you would like to submit your work to. The directions below explain each step in the process. In your activities notebook, put down your own answers to the questions. You can compile a separate form for each genre or area you are interested in.

Step 1. What is one of your favorite genres (take these from "The Wide World of Genres" activity in Chapter 3).

Step 2. Write in all the publishers of magazines or books that publish that genre. If you can't name any, go to some of the books or magazines that are in that genre, and take the publisher's name off the copyright page. The publisher's name or the name of one of their imprints is also on the spine of the jacket. It is always best to check the copyright page at the front of a book.

If you could only fill in only one publisher, you definitely need to become familiar with market guides (see Step 4 instructions).

Step 3. Write in the title of a piece of writing you are using for this exercise. Preferably, this would be a piece you want to have published or is a piece that is in the genre you want to

FINDING THE RIGHT PUBLISHER

Step 1 Favorite Genre:
Young Adult Novel

Step 2 Publishers:
Penguin, Avon, Scholastic

Step 3 Title of My Work:
Blue

Step 4 Publishers to Contact:
Avon, Delacorte, Scholastic

Step 5 Editor's Name
Avon — Ellen Krieger
Delacorte — check current Writer's Digest
Scholastic — ibid.

Step 6 Catalog
Sent for: Yes. (All 3.) November 15.
Received:
Avon — yes.
Delacorte — not yet.
Scholastic — yes.

be published in.

Step 4. Write in the publishers you would like to have this particular piece published by. Put in at least three. The emphasis or character of a particular publisher's list of books can be determined by looking at a recent catalog. Make sure you fit into the Publisher's Existing List. Now go back to Step 2 and double-check your list to make sure you haven't missed a potential market.

Step 5. Find the name of the editor who is responsible for your genre in the three publishing houses you have listed. Occasionally you can find the editor's name listed in a book's acknowledgments, particularly if the author felt that the editor was very good to work with. Most of the time, you can find the editor's name listed in the publisher's *Market Guide* listing.

Step 6. Write to the publishers you have selected in Step 4 and ask for their most recent catalog and writer's guidelines, if they have them. If you are approaching a publisher of a magazine, you should send for their guidelines. If you can't get a copy of the magazine from a local newsstand, they will usually send you a copy for a small fee plus postage.

Now you need to sort through all the information you have gathered. For a book publisher, study the catalog carefully. Does the type of books they publish really fit in with your work? If so, great. You have found a publisher you can keep an eye on for years to come. (Do watch out for changes, though, if the publisher gets bought by someone else!) If the catalog doesn't seem to fit what you had in mind, cross that name off your list and select another publisher to check out.

For a magazine publisher, study the magazine carefully. Does it really publish the type of articles you see yourself writing? If not, cross it off your list and find another.

What this exercise does is actually let you fine-tune your thinking about your writing and where you see it being published. For example, you may have had high hopes of publishing with the magazine *Seventeen*, only to find on reading the past year's short stories that they deal with more contemporary problems when you have an interest in historical fiction.

A Young Writers' Club

Once you have your publishing list set up, you can swap it with friends in your writing club, if you have one. If you are a really inventive group, why not come up with a permanent visual display of twenty to thirty publishers you have all targeted to be published with? You could make it like a Monopoly board, or any other board game you are familiar with. Fill in the publisher's name, address, the editor for different types of material, and the emphasis of the list. That way your club members can always refer to it.

Reading

To find out more about the publishing process, try consulting these books.

Appelbaum, Judith and Evans, Nancy. *How To Get Happily Published*. New York: Harper & Row, 1978.

Tomajczyk, S.F. *The Children's Writer's Marketplace*. Philadelphia: Running Press, 1987.

Turner, Barry, editor. *The Writer's Handbook*. London: Macmillan/Pen, 1989.

Various market guides are published by Writer's Digest Books. *The Poet's Market*, *The Writer's Market*, *The Song Writer's Market*, and *Novel and Short Story Market* are all updated annually. For a catalog, send to Writer's Digest Book Club, 1507 Dana Avenue, Cincinnati, OH 45207.

Chapter 6
Preparing Your Manuscript

The clock has just struck six o'clock. Jane, the fiction editor of Project X Publications, looks up at the clock and then back at the large pile of manuscript submissions sitting on her desk. She at least wants to have a glance at all of them before she leaves the office tonight.

She picks up the whole stack and moves over to a large conference table on which she can lay them out one by one and see what exactly is in her pile. Jane has worked as an editor for five years. She has learned how to weed the professional writing manuscripts from the unprofessional ones. She figures if the person sending the manuscript hasn't taken the time to prepare it properly, he probably hasn't taken much care with his manuscript.

She starts through the pile. The first submission has a one-page cover letter and a sample chapter. A quick glance shows that it is well-organized. It goes to the left side of the table—the potentials. The second submission has a five-page cover letter. On quick examination, the sample chapter is single-spaced and the type is so light, Jane has to squint to see it. She groans and wonders if writers ever think about how much editors have to read. She puts that submission to the right side of the table—the questionables.

Meanwhile, down the corridor from Jane, Rob, the nonfiction editor, is in his office looking at a large stack of nonfiction submissions. He quickly splits up the file to set aside for a closer look those submissions that have a cover letter outlining how long the book will be and when it will be ready for publication, in addition to being well-organized book proposals with brief outlines of each chapter and a sample chapter.

He is not happy to see full-length manuscripts with no book proposal. It means more work in trying to figure out if the book really has potential. He wonders if writers ever read the comments he puts every year in *The Writer's Market*. He also wonders if writers ever think what would make life easier for the editor.

One of the most important points for writers to learn is to be able to put yourself into the reader's shoes. Every time you submit a piece of writing—whether to your teacher, an editor, or whomever—keep the reader in mind. While you may understand clearly what your piece is about, to the reader your work is always new. It is information that has to be understood.

THE MANUSCRIPT PROPER

The following points should be followed for submitting your work to a publisher or an author who is critiquing your writing.

The Manuscript

Double-space your lines for all manuscripts, with the exception of poetry. To double-space your text, either set the line spacing of your typewriter to the number two, or on your word-processing program hit the keys for double-spacing.

Make sure you have used paragraphs. Do not hand in a short story or an article that is all one paragraph. Paragraphs are natural breaks in your writing. If you don't know what paragraphs are, ask your English teacher or parents for help.

If you have used dialogue in your story, make sure every time a new person speaks, a new paragraph begins. Enclose all dialogue in quotation marks.

Make sure each page is numbered clearly.

Make sure your spelling is correct. You can ask someone to proofread your work for you. If you use a spell-check program on your computer, remember they are not perfect. They just find the most common errors — and they don't know that you've used the wrong word.

Make sure your grammar is correct.

Avoid the overuse of a symbol such as *** to mark a break in a story. If you have too many, you may need to split up your piece into chapters.

Think of the front page as signaling to the reader everything they read to know: your name, address, telephone number, and social security number; the word count; the date; the title and the author.

The last page of your manuscript should let readers know they are at the end of your piece. At the end of your manuscript, drop down two lines and center the words "The End" or do what professional journalists do and use the number thirty (-30-).

Keep your manuscript simple, neat, and clean. Although it may seem strange to your creative urge, what works best in publishing is simple black type on white pages. Focus your attention on making your work easy to read. Avoid drawing on your poems, scribbling in margins, or using bizarre stationery! Any art should be submitted on separate pieces of paper.

Use good paper that can stand up to the test of being read a few times and passed around. Sixteen- to twenty-pound, white bond paper works well.

Use a paper clip or a long elastic band to hold your manuscript together. Don't staple or bind it together.

The Cover Letter

If you are submitting poems, short stories, articles, etc., for a contest, you don't need to send a cover letter. But if you are submitting any of your writing for normal publication, it is wise to send a cover letter.

This letter is like a regular letter. You want to write your name, address, telephone number, and date at the top. Then you want to write the name of the person you are sending it to, plus her address. If you can't find the person's name, put "Editor." Then begin your letter with the salutation "Dear Mr. or Ms."

Keep the letter brief and to the point. It should never be more than one page. State what you are sending, why, and how you see it fitting in with either their publication or their publishing list.

What Your Manuscript Should Not Look Like

SPLIT PEA SOUP
by
Christine Carriere

The setting for the whole dilemma was incredibly inap-
propriate. Glittering chandeliers, probably plastic, but I
thought at the time they were crystal; candlelit tables; em-
bossed wallpaper, and hidden air conditioners; not to mention
exotic prices. You are probably wondering what I was doing in
such a place alone. I had just been given a raise. After
months of careful planning, I had decided to celebrate. I had
ordered fish pate, and pecan pie for dessert. It only cost
$14.99; an amazing money-saver compared to numerous $29.99's,
and $45.99's that were offered for truffles and the like.
Anyway, I was thinking asterisks about the tardiness of my
food when I noticed a man two tables away from me wink
suggestively. "Ick!" I thought. "Half bald with wrinkles."
Even worse he had a peculiar taste for red wine and soup . . .
split pea. He took a sip from his soup spoon, swallowed, and
smiled

A Proper Manuscript First Page

Christine Carriere
597 2nd Street
London, Ontario
CANADA N2R 3X6
(519) 232-7788
SS# 000-00-000

About 1500 words
November 15, 1990

SPLIT PEA SOUP
by
Christine Carriere

The setting for the whole dilemma was incredibly inap-
propriate. Glittering chandeliers, probably plastic, but I
thought at the time they were crystal; candlelit tables; em-
bossed wallpaper, and hidden air conditioners; not to
mention exotic prices. You are probably wondering what I was
doing in such a place alone. I had just been given a raise.
After months of careful planning, I had decided to
celebrate. I had ordered fish pate, and pecan piece for
dessert. It only cost $14.99; an amazing money-saver
compared to numerous $29.99's, and $45.99's that were
offered for truffles and the like. Anyway, I was thinking
asterisks about the tardiness of my food when I noticed a
man two tables away from me wink suggestively.

"Ick!" I thought. "Half bald with wrinkles."

A Proper Manuscript Second Page

Carriere   SPLIT PEA SOUP   2

Even worse he had a peculiar taste for red wine and soup

. . . split pea. He took a sip from his soup spoon,

swallowed, and smiled widely and dipped his spoon again.

Suddenly, he shrieked, drawing the attention of the entire

patronage. He banged his spoon wildly on his water glass.

A Proper Cover Letter

```
Christine Carriere
597 2nd Street
London, Ontario
Canada N2R 3X6
(519) 232-7788

Nov. 20, 1990

The Editor
Great West Anthologies
P.O. Box 69
Vancouver, British Columbia
Canada V6G 2H1


Dear Editor:

I have enclosed a short story, Split Pea Soup, for consider-
ation in your anthology for young adults. I have read both
your 1988 and 1989 anthologies and feel this story would be
a natural fit for your 1991 version.

Yours sincerely,



Christine Carriere
```

The Envelope and the SASE

The last step is preparing the envelope and the SASE — self-addressed stamped envelope.

Choose two envelopes that are both big enough to hold your manuscript. A #10 business envelope will serve for manuscripts under four pages. Any manuscripts larger than that should be put into a 8½" x 11" envelope. You want the manuscript to slip out of the envelope at its destination looking as clean and crisp as it did at your end.

The first envelope is written to the person and publisher you are sending the manuscript. The second envelope, called

Sample Mailing Envelope

```
Christine Carriere                              Place
597 2nd St.                                     Stamp
London, Ontario                                 Here
N2R 3X6


                    The Editor
                    Great West Anthologies
                    P.O. Box 69
                    Vancouver, B.C.
                    V6G 2H1
```

Sample SASE

```
Great West Anthologies                          Place
P.O. Box 69                                     Stamp
Vancouver, B.C.                                 Here
V6G 2H1


                    Christine Carriere
                    597 2nd St.
                    London, Ontario
                    N2R 3X6
```

an SASE, is addressed from the publisher back to you. You need to place enough postage on it for your manuscript to be returned to you. Always remember to include an SASE. It saves the person receiving your manuscript or inquiry the trouble of typing up an envelope and the cost of the postage. As you can imagine, the cost of returning thousands of manuscripts would be tremendous, so this is why SASE's are used. If you don't include an SASE, your submission package will not be returned to you.

SUBMITTING A NOVEL

Read the entries in *The Writer's Digest* or *The Writer's Handbook* very carefully. Most editors will specify if they would like a brief synopsis of your novel with one, two, or three sample chapters. Take your sample chapters from different parts of the book. The first chapter should always be sent, along with a middle chapter and one at the end. Some editors like manuscripts in their entirety. This is especially true for children's books. If the editor has not made a specific entry, you can always call up the editor's secretary and ask what the normal procedure is for submitting a manuscript. Be brief and polite.

SUBMITTING A NONFICTION BOOK PROPOSAL

Unlike fiction, in which editors usually specify if they want a brief synopsis of your novel and one or two sample chapters, the nonfiction book proposal is a different kettle of fish.

A good nonfiction proposal contains the following five elements:

- A letter about the book.
- A working chapter outline.
- A summary of each chapter.
- A sample chapter.
- A marketing and competition summary.

In the letter about the book, you are expected to tell how many pages you expect the book to be. Check what seems to be the normal nonfiction lengths for adults and children. You'll be surprised to find that while there is some flexibility with page lengths, books especially for children have a certain range of pages. You can use the library/bookstore check. Just flip open books to the end and see how many pages there are.

You need to state when the manuscript will be finished, if it is not already completed. Books are published twice a year— in the spring and the fall. You will need to have your manuscript to the publisher at least six months before the expected publication date. Larger publishers usually require even longer than that.

You also should tell what the book is about. It helps to think about what the copy on the jacket of the book would be. Three or four very clear paragraphs will do.

A working chapter outline is like a table of contents on a school report or in a book. You may find it useful to examine the table of contents of either your favorite nonfiction books or nonfiction books dealing with the same topic you are writing about. You can also break down the chapters into subheads to give a clear idea of the book.

Working Chapter Outline

Daring to Begin: A Teenager's Guide to Developing Talent and Self-Esteem in ANY Career

1. Daring to Begin:
   Why Your Life Can't Wait until You Finish School
2. Your Ticket to Ride:
   When Who You Are Is NOT Your School Marks
3. Turn It On:
   How to Develop Your Own Talent
4. Dynamite!
   Four Simple Tricks to Blast Your Way through Homework and Projects
5. Let's Make a Deal:
   How to Get Support from Parents, Mentors and Friends
6. Something Important to Do:
   How to Invent Your Own Life

A summary of each chapter should consist of one or two

paragraphs about the main points in each chapter. Be very concise but precise here. This may require re-writing quite a few times.

Sample: A Summary of Chapter One

CHAPTER ONE
Daring to Begin:
Why Your Life Can't Wait Until You Finish School

"Behold the turtle. He makes progress only when he sticks his neck out."
James Bryant Conant

There are certain myths that hold teenagers back from stepping out to develop their own lives—myths such as a teenager cannot take control of their education or get a job that is interesting or gives them the necessary experience. In this chapter, teenagers explore why it is better to take control of their own life as opposed to being a "victim" of the system. They also find out why their talent may not be obvious to them and why it is important to start taking steps now to develop their own talent.

For a sample chapter, take the best chapter you have or the one you think conveys the idea of the book the best. Follow all the rules about preparing a manuscript (double-spaced, etc.).

A marketing and competition summary is a one-page document explaining why you think the book will sell and why you are the best person to write it. It should also list any other books that are similar to yours and why you think yours is different from and better than the others.

 **ACTIVITIES**

Publication Record

Remember to keep track of where you have sent your manuscripts so that you can follow up on the replies you get from publishers.

Here is a sample of a simple way you can keep track of where your submissions are. 3" x 5" index cards filed in a box are an easy way to organize your records. Keep a sheet or index card for each manuscript you send out. Record the name of the story or article you sent out. Put down the publisher you sent it to. Write the date you sent it and what sort of response you got.

> Record of Submission: Year 1991
> Title: Split Pea Soup
> Date Sent: January 19, 1991
> Sent to: Highlights
> Their Reply: Rejected
> Date: April 20, 1991

Submitting It Right Checklist

You now have a manuscript, a cover letter, and two envelopes in your hand. Look at this list and make sure you have everything in order properly.

- A publishable manuscript, checked for spelling and grammar mistakes.
- A self-addressed stamped envelope so the publisher can return your manuscript.
- You are sending it to the right publisher and the right editor.
- A record of when you send out your manuscripts. Keep

this record in the front of the file you keep on each manuscript you are trying to sell.

- Optional: Attach a biographical sheet.

Making Your Own Bio Sheet

This activity is really looking into the future when a bio sheet will become a necessity for interviews, articles on your writing, etc. You may find it useful to pique the interest of an editor with some of your writing accomplishments. Rather than writing up the same information every time, it saves time to have a standard bio sheet that you can photocopy and send out with your submissions. Make sure you update it each time you have a piece published or have an accomplishment that would be worth noting.

Again, like your manuscript submissions, black ink on white paper works best. A good black and white photo of you is also a bonus.

Essential ingredients to include are:

- A good photo of yourself;
- Your home address and phone number;
- Your school or university;
- Your memberships in clubs, organizations, etc.;
- Your published works;
- Any special awards or experience;
- Magazines or newspapers you write articles for;
- Writing workshops attended.

Reading

To find out more about submitting your writing, try reading Lisa Cool Collier's, *How to Write Irresistible Query Letters* (Cincinnati: Writer's Digest, 1990).

Chapter 7
Being Smart about Your Money and Your Rights

Everyone has different ideas about how much money a writer makes. There are stories of well-known authors who make millions of dollars from their books. (Stephen King and Danielle Steel — to name two.) Then there are stories of both well-known and little-known authors who have made or make little money. (All the way from Charles Dickens to most living poets.)

To further complicate things, depending on the culture you live in, it may be okay or not okay to talk about money. And then there are all sorts of sayings like, "Money doesn't grow on trees" and "The starving-artist syndrome." As you sit there wondering how much a short story or a poem or a novel you have just written will make, or wondering how much money you could make once you graduate, or how do you make a million dollars from a book, take all that natural curiosity you have about money and make a promise to yourself to always be curious about money.

By being curious about money, always asking questions, understanding how you get paid (flat fees and royalties), and reading nonfiction books on money, you will teach yourself to be financially *intelligent* — one of the greatest gifts you can give yourself to ensure becoming a successful writer.

The financial information in this chapter is divided into two sections. "How Writers Get Paid" is designed to answer the most common questions of young writers, how much writers receive for a piece of writing, when payment occurs, and other factors involved in payments. The examples involve very simple multiplication, division, and percentages. If you haven't learned how to do this type of math at school yet, ask your parents or a friend to help you. You can use a calculator or financial spreadsheets if you have a computer and spreadsheet software program.

"Making Sound Financial Decisions" is designed to help young writers who have to make sensible career decisions. The examples include much more advanced calculation sheets. The purpose of these calculation sheets is to make you familiar with budgets and cash flow forecast sheets. Want to convince your parents that you have a sensible financial plan for becoming a writer? Read this section.

In order to be as wealthy as you want to be, you need just three things: 1. A clear vision of what you want. 2. The belief you will get it. 3. Practical skills to put that belief into action.

Jerry Gillies, author of Moneylove

SCHOOL AND FINANCIAL SKILLS

You may be surprised at the number of different subjects at school that can help your writing career. In your math class you learn how to add, subtract, divide, multiply, and calculate *percentages*. In geography you are taught about the major industries of the world. If you have the opportunity to do a project of your own choosing, you might examine if the book industry is a major industry in your own country and write a report on it. In your economics course you learn about the theory of supply and demand and how it differs in different markets. Think about how books, magazines, plays, etc., are sold in your country. And, of course, there are accounting and law, both of which help you become very smart about your money and your rights.

FINANCES

In the beginning of your writing career, the joy of just being published and making some extra pocket money will be immensely satisfying to you. You may find a short story of yours has been chosen for an anthology and you are $200 richer. Or you have sold three nonfiction articles to various magazines for a total of $150.

When you know that a typical youth is able to make anywhere from $4 to $10 an *hour* working in a part-time job, these larger sums of money can cause you to ask some interesting and very important questions.

- Should I be spending more time writing?
- How many stories and articles could I sell if I really put my mind to it this year?
- How much money can I really make from my writing?
- Should I keep my part-time job and put time aside to write?
- And for those of you looking far down the road—How many books and articles does one have to write and sell a year to make a living?

The first concern for youth is, "What do I do when I graduate?" The second concern is money. Most teenagers are almost totally dependent on the financial support of their parents. You may have a part-time job that allows you to buy personal items or to save for a larger, important item (a car, college, etc.). But you know that once school is over, you will be responsible for making the money (income) to cover what you need to live (expenses).

HOW WRITERS GET PAID

One benefit of an hourly paid job is in knowing exactly how much money you are getting each week you work. For example, if you have planned to buy a second-hand computer for $400, and you manage to save $20 a week from a part-time job, you know it will take twenty weeks of saving to reach your goal. The good thing about an hourly job is that you can count on that money every week. A potential drawback of an hourly paid job is that in order to increase the amount of money you make, you will need to do something else. You need to increase the amount of hours you work, get a promotion to a higher paying job, get a raise, or even find another job that pays a higher hourly rate.

Writers are rarely paid an hourly rate. Writers are paid in one of three ways: a rate per word, a flat rate, or royalties. Each piece of writing they do will usually command a different sum of money. For example, a 1,000 word article on camping for one magazine paying ten cents a word would result in a $100 check. The same article to a newspaper paying a flat rate of $150 an article would result in a $150 check. An adventure book based on your experiences camping is picked up by a children's publisher paying a 10% royalty. The book sells for $4.95. The royalty per book would be .495. If your book sells 5,000 copies, you will make roughly $2,500 (5,000 x .495).

The benefit of being paid in any of these ways is that in the long run you can make more money per hour than you ever could being an hourly paid worker. For example, one of your books may become a modest bestseller, and the six months of work you put in to write the book may bring you a far greater amount of money over the next five years than you could have ever earned in an hourly job working for six months.

The potential drawbacks are, one, your book may not make a lot of money, and two, it is difficult to predict accurately how much money you will make. One year, you may have a good year, covering your living expenses and making a profit. Another year, you may have a slow year, just making enough money to cover your basic living expenses.

While magazine writers, who are paid a flat fee or rate per word, have a slightly easier time of predicting how much money will come in, authors who are paid by the sales of their books never know exactly how much money is coming in until their publisher issues them a royalty statement (usually every six months).

Read through each section carefully. If you have any difficulties, try going over them with a friend or even a parent. Look at it this way. Your parents will be impressed that you are learning sound financial skills and that you are being realistic. At least your decisions can have some financial reality backing them up.

PAYMENT

Payment by the Word

Payment by the word, *per word* in professional jargon, most often applies to magazine writing. When you have received the guidelines you sent away for, they should tell you the payment terms of the magazine: how much they pay, when they pay, and what rights they buy.

As an example, imagine you have written a 300-word article on baseball for *Young American*. Since it pays 7 cents per word, your 300-word article will earn you $21. Another important factor is when they pay that money. In this case, they pay upon publication of the article, so you may not see your money for a few months after it has been accepted. Other magazines may pay on acceptance, which means you will receive your money right away. This can be very important to a writer—especially one who is just starting out as a full-time freelancer!

Flat Fee

Another common way magazines pay is with a *flat fee*. This type of payment may apply to short stories, single poems, articles, and even certain books. It can range from free copies of a book or magazine to thousands of dollars for top magazines.

Imagine you have written a personal essay for *Careers Magazine*. They pay a flat fee, which their guidelines state is $50. Once again, this may be paid on acceptance or on publication.

Royalties

For most books—fiction, poetry, and nonfiction—you are paid according to the number of copies of your book that is sold. Royalty rates can differ according to the country you are published in and the type of book being published (hardcover, trade paperback, and mass market paperback).

Here is an example. You have written a young adult novel. It sells for $4.95. You have agreed to receive a 10% royalty. First, take the price of the book and calculate what 10% of that price is.

What you now have is .495—the basic royalty amount you,

the author, will get for each book sold. If 5,000 copies are sold, the author will make $2,500. If 10,000 copies are sold, the author will make $5,000.

To go one step further, if you want to make this exercise relevant to your own field, take a published book that is both from a publisher on your selected list (Chapter 5) and roughly the same type of book you are writing. Now, do the royalty calculation based on its cover price.

On a more special note, if you write a picture book and an illustrator illustrates your book, you normally split your royalties fifty-fifty.

Royalties are usually paid twice a year. But this changes according to the publisher and will be specified on your contract.

FINANCING YOUR WRITING

A typical book gets signed one year and published the next, with royalty checks starting the following year (if sales exceed the advances). For example: A book contract signed in 1993 would most likely be published in 1994, and you would start seeing royalty checks (depending on your sales) in 1995.

What happens if you have a great idea for a book? You've written either the first three chapters of a piece of fiction or you've done a fifty-page nonfiction book proposal complete with a sample chapter. The publisher loves the idea, and you are excited about writing the book, except for the question of what you are going to do for money during the six or nine months it takes to write the rest of the book. In publishing circles, there is a type of payment up-front for work done on a book. It is called an advance.

Advance

An advance is what the publisher pays you up-front before your book is published. Ideally, it is supposed to cover your expenses in writing the book. For beginning writers, it rarely does.

An advance can be 50% of the royalties on the first print run of your book. Half the advance is usually paid when you sign the contract, and the other half when the manuscript is complete.

For example: Your book is selling for $10 and your royalties are $1 a book. Say 5,000 copies are printed on the first print run. 5,000 books x $1 royalty equals $5,000. So, 50% of your first print run is $5,000 divided by two, which equals $2,500. You would only get half of that advance before you wrote the book, so during the six months to write the book you would have $1,225.

If you have a book that will take six months to write, $1,225 divided by six equals approximately $200. Whether or not that $200 will cover your living expenses depends on what living expenses you have, whether you are paying rent, providing your own food, etc. Most likely, $200 a month is not enough to support yourself.

It is not until you've made a reputation for yourself that you will be entitled to larger advances. The reason is that as you develop a track record as an author whose books sell, the publisher is less at risk in publishing your book. The predicted sales are higher and therefore your advance is higher too. This is why some authors always have another source of income or a savings account to back them up during tough times.

Other Forms of Income

You now understand why most authors must make money from different types of activities. Advances and royalties are just two sources of income. Other sources of income include:

- government or private agency grants;
- public lending right (payment for use of your books in the library);
- awards;
- freelance writing — magazines, newspapers, book reviews;
- speaking at conferences;
- leading workshops;
- reading from your book in a school or library;
- holding another paying job.

MAKING SOUND FINANCIAL DECISIONS

As you move from being a beginning writer earning extra

pocket money from the sale of your writing, to wanting to earn a good part-time income, and eventually to wanting to earn a good full-time income, your financial skills need to become increasingly better.

As you have seen already, every author takes a financial risk. With a bit of foresight and planning, you can choose to avoid the most common financial mistakes young entrepreneurs have made. One is not keeping a simple budget (cash flow forecast and income and expenses sheet). The second is overspending, such as buying purchases on credit cards.

Since this is a more complicated section, there are several requirements to keep in mind. First, you will need to know how to add, subtract, multiply, and divide. You can use a calculator or a computer spreadsheet such as Lotus.

Make sure you understand each section before you move on to the next. If you don't, ask your parents or a teacher at school to help you.

Finally, give yourself plenty of time to work through this section and don't rush through it. You can do one step at a time. Do make sure you understand one part before you begin another.

BUDGETS

A budget includes income, expenses, and savings. A personal finance plan includes a budget, short-term goals, and long-term goals.

Your income is the money you have coming in from your part-time job, allowance, or special gifts of money.

Expenses are money you pay out for regular expenses and irregular expenses. *Fixed expenses* are regular expenses. After high school, one of your largest fixed expenses is accommodation. They would also include food, electricity, telephone, and savings. *Flexible expenses* are expenses that are irregular. They can be large or small expenses. For example, a second-hand computer, a Walkman™, books, magazines, movies, computer paper, memberships, gifts, etc.

Catriona's Budget

Catriona is sixteen years old. She works part-time ten

hours a week in a local bookstore, one evening and one Saturday a week. She makes $5 an hour. Her monthly income from her job is $200.

Catriona has never done a budget. She lives to spend some of her money on clothes, books, albums, and going out with her friends. She saves $50 a month.

CATRIONA'S ONE MONTH BUDGET

	Column 1	Column 2	Column 3
INCOME			
Allowance	$10	$10	$10
Job	$200	$200	$200
Gift	$0	$0	$0
TOTAL INCOME	$210	$210	$210
EXPENSES			
Fixed			
Savings	$50	$100	$110
Flexible			
Clothes	?$50	$30	$30
Books	$10	$25	$25
Computer Paper	$10	$10	$10
Records	?$20	$10	$0
Entertainment	?	$25	$25
Gifts	?	$10	$10
TOTAL EXPENSES	$140	$210	$210

Catriona sits down to fill in what she thinks she spends a month. She is surprised to see that there is $70 she cannot account for. These figures are given in the first column of her budget.

In the second column, Catriona fills in what she would like to spend on certain items. She has a short list of short-term goals. Her three goals are to save for a second-hand computer, which costs $600; the cost of a writing workshop, $100; and her own library of reference books and favorite authors, $25 a month.

In order to achieve these goals, she has increased her savings enough to cover a computer and the workshop. She has also increased her budget for the amount of books she wants to purchase. She has reduced the number of records she will buy a month.

In the third column, Catriona has totaled her receipts for the month. She has kept pretty much to her budget, with one exception. There wasn't a record that interested her that month, so she put $10 extra into her savings account.

Catriona's Budget Ten Years Later

Catriona is now twenty-six. Consult the figure to see what her budget looks like for the first six months.

As for her income, she has a full-time job and her take-home pay each month (after taxes) is $1,500. She has kept her hand in at writing the occasional magazine article, and just this year, she signed her first book contract in April. Catriona has a good sense of both her fixed and flexible expenses. She keeps her business expenses separate from her personal expenses.

Cash Flow Forecasts

A cash flow forecast allows you to see what would happen if you dropped one source of income, or added one source of income. In order to make a good decision you need to know if you could still cover your existing expenses. (It can also be used to let you see what happens if you reduce one or two expenses.)

Catriona is considering whether to keep her full-time job or go into writing full-time.

In Cash Flow Forecast #1, Catriona takes away the income from her job to see how much and what sort of action she would need to take. She sees that she would have to replace almost half her full-time income, by selling more of her writing, to cover her expenses.

In Cash Flow Forecast #2, Catriona has managed to land a regular column with a magazine. This income — $1,200 a month — will replace most of the income she makes if she leaves her job. This is what her financial picture would look like.

Catriona decides to hold onto her job and her regular column for another year. She wants to build up a good savings

CATRIONA'S SIX-MONTH BUDGET AT AGE TWENTY-SIX

	Jan.	Feb.	March	April	May	June	Total
Previous Month's Balance	0.00	910.83	1,266.66	2,277.49	3,688.32	4,498.82	
INCOME							
Magazines	500.00	0.00	500.00	0.00	500.00	0.00	1,500.00
Books	0.00	0.00	0.00	1,000.00	0.00	0.00	1,000.00
Job	1,500.00	1,500.00	1,500.00	1,500.00	1,500.00	1,500.00	9,000.00
Total Income	2,000.00	1,500.00	2,000.00	2,500.00	2,000.00	1,500.00	11,500.00
Adjusted Balance	2,000.00	2,410.83	3,266.66	4,777.49	5,688.32	5,998.82	
EXPENSES							
Personal							
Food	150.00	150.00	150.00	150.00	150.00	150.00	900.00
Rent (75%)	225.00	225.00	225.00	225.00	225.00	225.00	1,350.00
Health	50.00	50.00	50.00	50.00	50.00	50.00	300.00
Clothes	100.00	0.00	0.00	100.00	0.00	0.00	200.00
Savings	100.00	100.00	100.00	100.00	100.00	100.00	600.00
Car Insurance	94.17	94.17	94.17	94.17	179.50	89.75	645.93
Car	210.00	210.00	210.00	210.00	210.00	210.00	1,260.00
Gas	20.00	20.00	20.00	20.00	20.00	20.00	120.00
Home Office							
Prof. Fees	0.00	55.00	0.00	0.00	0.00	50.00	105.00
Convention	0.00	0.00	0.00	0.00	115.00	0.00	115.00
Entertainment	0.00	100.00	0.00	0.00	0.00	0.00	100.00
Telephone	20.00	20.00	20.00	20.00	20.00	20.00	120.00
Office Exp.	20.00	20.00	20.00	20.00	20.00	20.00	120.00
Rent (25%)	75.00	75.00	75.00	75.00	75.00	75.00	450.00
Library	25.00	25.00	25.00	25.00	25.00	25.00	150.00
Total Expenses	1,089.17	1,144.17	989.17	1089,17	1089.50	1034.75	6,535.93
BALANCE	910.83	1,266.66	2,277.49	3,688.32	4,498.82	4,964.07	4,964.07

CATRIONA'S CASH FLOW FORECAST IF SHE LEFT HER JOB

	Jan.	Feb.	March	April	May	June	Total
Previous Month's Balance	0.00	-589.17	-1,733.34	-2,222.51	-2,311.68	-3,001.18	
INCOME							
Magazines	500.00	0.00	500.00	0.00	500.00	0.00	1,500.00
Books	0.00	0.00	0.00	1,000.00	0.00	0.00	1,000.00
Total Income	500.00	0.00	500.00	1,000.00	500.00	0.00	2,500.00
Adjusted Balance	500.00	-589.17	-1,233.34	-1,222.51	-1,811.68	-3,001.18	
EXPENSES							
Personal							
Food	150.00	150.00	150.00	150.00	150.00	150.00	900.00
Rent (75%)	225.00	225.00	225.00	225.00	225.00	225.00	1,350.00
Health	50.00	50.00	50.00	50.00	50.00	50.00	300.00
Clothes	100.00	0.00	0.00	100.00	0.00	0.00	200.00
Savings	100.00	100.00	100.00	100.00	100.00	100.00	600.00
Car Insurance	94.17	94.17	94.17	94.17	179.50	89.75	645.93
Car	210.00	210.00	210.00	210.00	210.00	210.00	1,260.00
Gas	20.00	20.00	20.00	20.00	20.00	20.00	120.00
Home Office							
Prof. Fees	0.00	55.00	0.00	0.00	0.00	50.00	105.00
Convention	0.00	0.00	0.00	0.00	115.00	0.00	115.00
Entertainment	0.00	100.00	0.00	0.00	0.00	0.00	100.00
Telephone	20.00	20.00	20.00	20.00	20.00	20.00	120.00
Office Exp.	20.00	20.00	20.00	20.00	20.00	20.00	120.00
Rent (25%)	75.00	75.00	75.00	75.00	75.00	75.00	450.00
Library	25.00	25.00	25.00	25.00	25.00	25.00	150.00
Total Expenses	1,089.17	1,144.17	989.17	1089,17	1089.50	1034.75	6,535.93
BALANCE	-589.17	-1,733.34	-2,222.51	-2,311.68	-3,001.18	-4,035.93	-4,035.93

CATRIONA'S CASH FLOW FORECAST IF SHE LEFT HER JOB (REVISED)

	Jan.	Feb.	March	April	May	June	Total
Previous Month's Balance	0.00	110.83	166.66	377.49	2,488.32	2,498.82	
INCOME							
Magazines	1,200.00	1,200.00	1,200.00	1,200.00	1,200.00	1,200.00	7,200.00
Books	0.00	0.00	0.00	2,000.00	0.00	0.00	2,000.00
Adjusted Balance	1,200.00	1,310.83	1,366.66	3,577.49	3,688.32	3,698.82	
EXPENSES							
Personal							
Food	150.00	150.00	150.00	150.00	150.00	150.00	900.00
Rent (75%)	225.00	225.00	225.00	225.00	225.00	225.00	1,350.00
Health	50.00	50.00	50.00	50.00	50.00	50.00	300.00
Clothes	100.00	0.00	0.00	100.00	0.00	0.00	200.00
Savings	100.00	100.00	100.00	100.00	100.00	100.00	600.00
Car Insurance	94.17	94.17	94.17	94.17	179.50	89.75	645.93
Car	210.00	210.00	210.00	210.00	210.00	210.00	1,260.00
Gas	20.00	20.00	20.00	20.00	20.00	20.00	120.00
Home Office							
Prof. Fees	0.00	55.00	0.00	0.00	0.00	50.00	105.00
Convention	0.00	0.00	0.00	0.00	115.00	0.00	115.00
Entertainment	0.00	100.00	0.00	0.00	0.00	0.00	100.00
Telephone	20.00	20.00	20.00	20.00	20.00	20.00	120.00
Office Exp.	20.00	20.00	20.00	20.00	20.00	20.00	120.00
Rent (25%)	75.00	75.00	75.00	75.00	75.00	75.00	450.00
Library	25.00	25.00	25.00	25.00	25.00	25.00	150.00
Total Expenses	1,089.17	1,144.17	989.17	1089,17	1089.50	1034.75	6,535.93
BALANCE	110.83	166.66	377.49	2,488.32	2,498.82	2,664.07	2,664.07

account. She makes a note to do a cash flow next year at the same time and see if she would like to risk being a full-time writer then.

SAVINGS

Why save? You are probably already saving for college or to move out on your own and work. Yet one of the most important reasons for having a separate savings account may not have crossed your mind. If you want to purchase a major item that involves taking out a bank loan, you will be able to get a loan and good interest terms if you can secure the loan with a healthy savings account. For example, if you want to borrow $3,000, you should have $1,000 in a savings account. Most financial planners will tell you never to take on a debt load ratio of more than three to one.

It is a good idea to get into the habit of planning your financial income even as a part-time beginning writer. What you will see is that each month you get a different amount of money. Each month you may receive a different sum of money depending on grants, royalty checks, payment for a poem or an article, an award, etc.

Computers and Modems

Probably one of the most important purchases to be planned for in your writing career, and one which a proper savings plan will allow you, is a computer. It is not essential if you are writing poetry but it is certainly helpful for any fiction or non-fiction. A computer is an important writing tool because it saves time.

With a word processing program you don't need to rewrite everything from scratch as soon as you make one mistake. With a spreadsheet program, the computer keeps your budgets and does all your math for you.

Computers don't need to be costly purchases. One of the boys attending my camp purchased a wonderful second-hand portable computer for a fraction of its original price.

LEARN MORE FINANCIAL SKILLS

You can see from the previous financial sheets that unless

one has a private income, most writers either get a full-time job that involves writing or get a job that pays their bills and pursue their writing in their own spare time. The reading you did in Chapter 1 on your favorite authors may have given you some ideas on how to fit writing into your life in your adult years.

I highly recommend that you copy the sheets in this chapter *or* take an accounting course at school *or* learn how to do a budget with your parents *or* learn how to use a spreadsheet (a computer program that automatically calculates rows of sums for you). Most banks have free pamphlets on various aspects of personal financing. See if your local bank has a pamphlet on budgets.

In the future, you can explore the possibility of starting your own part-time business. Most adult writers are in business for themselves—either part-time or full-time. The advantages to actually starting a business as a writer is that you can deduct some of your expenses from your income, thereby reducing your overall income tax. (Watch out for different tax rules in different countries.)

You now know some of the basics about how a writer gets paid. May you make all the sensible financial decisions you need to ensure that you have a healthy writing life.

RIGHTS

One of the first words to learn regarding your rights as a writer is the word "copyright." Copyright is the term for ownership of a piece of writing. It is signified by the symbol ©. Your writing is "yours" until fifty years after you die, unless you decide to sell your copyright, or ownership of the piece. (Note: Copyright laws may be different in each country. Check out the copyright laws in your own country.)

Selling your copyright is usually the last thing you want to do. If a certain magazine or publisher is asking you to give up your copyright, you have two choices. Look for another place to be published, or talk to a professional writing organization and see if you have any other options.

When you write any piece of writing for a magazine, they usually buy one of two rights (not your copyright): First Serial

Rights or Second Serial Rights (Reprint Rights). First Serial Rights give the magazine the right to publish the article for the *first* time in any magazine. Second Serial Rights give the magazine the right to publish the piece after it has appeared in another magazine. Second Serial Rights also apply to a magazine excerpting part of a book after it has been published, regardless of whether it has been printed in another magazine first.

CONTRACTS

A contract is a complex legal document. It is the document you are asked to sign when you are giving a publisher the right to publish your work. The publisher's editor gives you the house's "standard" publishing contract when the publisher wishes to publish your book. Unfortunately for the beginning writer, no two publishers have the same contract, and if you have no experience in negotiating or understanding legal documents, you are not in a good bargaining position.

Fortunately, almost all professional writing organizations in most countries around the world have some guidelines for understanding contracts. Even if you are exceptionally bright and used to handling problems by yourself, the legal implications of every clause in a contract can take months (if not years) to really get a grasp on if you try to do it by yourself.

Since contracts can run anywhere from five pages to twenty-five or more pages, and contracts change according to which country you live in, the best advice I can give you is to order a set of guidelines from your local writing organization when the mood takes you to have a look at a writer's contract.

If you get an offer on a contract on a book, play, book of poems, or anything, contact the relevant organization in your country. (See the list of writing organizations in Chapter 8.)

Receiving a Contract

Almost all beginning writers (unless they come from a family of bankers or lawyers) think a contract is written in stone. Contracts can frequently be negotiated. You especially want to be sure you understand what money you are making off your book and what subsidiary rights you will have a say in.

Many contracts have been signed by beginning writers in a rush, only to be found at a later date not to contain the requirements the author really wanted. When you receive a contract, take a deep breath, because you have to switch from your creative hat to your business hat. Then follow the steps below.

One, read the contract. Never sign it on receiving it in the editor's office. In reality, the contract will probably take a week to a month to understand, possibly negotiate, and sign. Don't rush in your excitement. (Note: If you are under eighteen, in most countries your parents will need to sign the contract with you.)

Two, get out your guide to contracts from your local writing organization. Mark clauses that are okay with a check. Anything (and I mean anything) you have a question about, mark with a question mark.

Three, call the staff person in charge of contracts. He will help you understand the clauses you are not clear about. Before you do so, be certain that you have read it carefully and learned everything you can about publishing contracts. Don't ask silly questions that you would understand if you had read the contract extremely closely and done a little research.

Four, prepare a list of what you really want in the contract (money, ratio regarding rights, etc.). If you decide it is vital that you negotiate a better contract, remember to be polite and diplomatic in your negotiations. Don't expect that you will get your way as soon as you state "Give me a better contract or I won't sign it." The publishing company may simply wish you luck elsewhere. Give solid, legitimate reasons to support your claims.

RULE OF THUMB: *Never* sign a book contract without first talking to a staff person in a professional writing organization, your lawyer, or your agent.

Don't Suffer in Silence

One of the most important things to remember is not to suffer in silence. If you can't figure out what a clause in a contract means, or you've submitted a piece and never been paid properly for it, or someone assumed copyright of your piece, *immediately* get in touch with one of the professional writing associations listed in Chapter 8.

To find out more about making money and signing contracts, read:

Gillies, Jerry. *Moneylove: How to Get the Money You Deserve for Whatever You Want.* New York: Warner, 1978.

Answers to Some Questions About Contracts. The Society of Children's Book Writers.

Help Yourself to a Better Contract. The Writers' Union of Canada.

Temple, Todd. *How to Become a Teenage Millionaire.* Nashville: Thomas Nelson, Inc., 1991.

✎_____**ACTIVITIES**

Write Your Own Budget

Using Catriona's budget as a guide, write your own budget in your activities notebook. Using the past month as a guide, fill in the first column as best you can. You may be surprised, as Catriona was and many other people are, that there is a large sum of money you can't account for. Then fill out in the second column the budget you would like to follow for the next month. Remember to include a figure for your savings account.

Keep all your receipts for one month. At the end of that month, fill in the third column. How did you do? Are there any changes that need to be made to the second column for your budget to work for you?

Running out of your allowance midweek may not be a big issue right now, but it may be a sign of poor planning, which can lead to dangerous habits in the future when you are responsible for all of your expenses.

Look at a budget as a logical way to help you spend your money on what you really want and to keep you from throwing your money away on things you don't really want. Once you know where you are spending your money, it will be much easier to meet your payments and have money for your short- and long-term goals.

Chapter 8

Reaching Out: Linking Up with the Writing Community

In the past I tried discussing the art of capturing good dialogue and outrageous characters at parties, only to be shunned to the vegetable and dip table. I was a closet writer.

Christine, age eighteen

Nature's answer to having a small number of writers in a school or community is guaranteeing that an interest in writing transcends all the normal age barriers. Having conversations with people about the things we find interesting is vital for development. While engaged in conversations with people, all sorts of new possibilities can emerge. A chance comment to a friend about the fact that you want to find a writing class may turn up the contact name you've been looking for. A question to your teacher about needing more interesting books may take you to a new section of the library.

The conversations you have, not only with yourself, but with other people, can be one of the most important tools for becoming a writer. For it is in conversations that you make promises to yourself to do certain things by a certain time. It is in conversations that you make requests of people (for example, ask people to help you find an address). It is in conversations that you make declarations, like "I am a writer," which serve as launching pads for future actions.

While it takes a bit of effort to find other young writers, the reward is well worth it. It takes effort because most young writers are isolated in their schools or communities. It also takes effort because writing clubs are not available in every community to the same extent that ice rinks or baseball fields are.

Christine found new writing friends at a summer camp. Other young writers have found friends at a local writing club, a drama workshop, working part-time in a library, etc. Other ways that young writers have found each other are by:

- Attending a young writers' workshop.
- Attending a local professional writers' meeting.
- Working on a school or youth community newspaper.
- Writing for a pen pal through special young authors' magazines.
- Attending a local adult writers' workshop (which you need permission to attend).
- Asking an English teacher, drama teacher, or librarian if she knows of other young writers in the school. You may not know these people because they are not in your class or your grade.

WORKING WITH OTHER YOUNG WRITERS

All writers have their own unique gifts to bring to the world. Given that writers come from different backgrounds and different schools, all writers (young and old) are at a different stage with their writing. It helps as you enter the world of writing to forget about grades and about competing with each other. You have more power if your focus stays on what you are working on. If you are working on a science fiction novel for the Avon competition two years away, there is not much point in being concerned about competing with Angie, who has finished a short story and has already submitted it to *Reader's Digest*. Even if your friend Mark is also working on a realistic novel for the Avon competition, you will find that supporting each other to write the best novel possible will be far more inspiring.

The real power in friendship is looking for what you can contribute to each other without keeping score. Does Angie need some encouragement to start her next short story? Does Mark need some encouragement to spend some time home writing tonight? Would Trudi like to borrow your book on developing plots in science fiction?

Professional authors focus on creating the best work possible and getting it published, not on competition with other authors.

Other Artists

Other artists are also potential friends. In the United States, the Society of Children's Book Writers has both authors and illustrators as members. In Canada, the Canadian Society of Children's Authors, Illustrators and Performers has all three types of artists as members, making it one of the most unusual artists' organizations for children's culture in the world! Both organizations recognize the tremendous benefit in having artists of different disciplines meet and share their ideas together.

One wonderful example of talented people sharing their creativity, even though they were involved in many different areas, was The Bloomsbury Group. The Bloomsbury Group had Thursday night meetings at the turn of the twentieth century. The original group consisted of Maynard Keynes (economist), Virginia Woolf, Leonard Woolf (Virginia's husband and a political scientist), Lytton Strachey (biographer), Duncan Grant, Vanessa Bell (Virginia's sister-in-law), and Roger Fry (painters). Some of the visitors to the group were T.S. Eliot, Bertrand Russell, and E.M. Forster.

YOURSELF

Most young writers are incredibly independent and self-sufficient. As you read through the five suggestions below, keep in mind that these might be areas that your friends or a parent can help you with. Your family or friends who are not writers, and therefore may feel they don't have much to offer you in helping you become a writer, may be thrilled to help you with the following:

Your Own Writing Room

One of the things you might like to start doing right now is designing a proper writing room.

When you have an idea you care about strongly enough to

want to write a book about it, keep everything you find related to it in a special colored three-ring binder. (If you are working on a computer, you can keep the print-out in the binder.) I use different colors as a code, e.g., blue for nonfiction and pink for fiction.

I find it a great help to always visualize the book as completed. I usually put a favorite comic on the front cover to inspire me.

You can use file folders to keep brochures and other awkward items that won't fit into a three-ring binder. A small filing cabinet or a set of wire baskets is useful for organizing all your material.

Use your room to inspire you. The original artwork of my book covers goes up on my wall, along with favorite reviews. You can put up important quotes and posters of new books. Use anything that works to inspire you! (My friend, author and illustrator Mark Thurman, has a skeleton in his workroom!)

Be Environmentally Friendly

Try some of the following, if you don't already. Use both sides of your paper. In your room, have two baskets—one for paper to be recycled and one for things that can't be recycled. Adopt an endangered species (plant or animal), perhaps one that people don't know about in your local area. Write articles about it. When you need wrapping paper for special occasions, make your own from cartoons in the newspaper, pictures from magazines, or old calendars.

Your Own Personalized Library

The greatest part of a writer's time is spent in reading; in order to write, a man will turn over half a library to make one book.

Samuel Johnson.

Start your own unique library of books. You can collect

autographed books of favorite authors, or collect second-hand copies of rare books. Remember, buying books supports the industry you wish to enter.

Get subscriptions to magazines you are interested in being published with. (Check them out at the library first if you are not familiar with them.)

To read fine books is as necessary to a writer as water is to a fish. The need to supplement most academic programs, whether at the high school or college level, is a prerequisite for young writers who are serious about writing. Nothing can be more frustrating than having time on one's hands to do lots of reading and being unable to find good books.

Most young writers are eager for new books to read. Books that challenge their beliefs. Books with characters that transport you to another time period. Books that teach you about humanity 100, 200, or 2,000 years ago. Books that grapple with issues that are fundamental to being human.

Good books are available. The trick is knowing the titles, the authors, and where to find them. Try reading some of the classics — Plato, Tolstoy, George Eliot. The books called the "classics" become art, are immortal, and stay around for hundreds of years because they are so astoundingly good that people don't want to forget them.

If you live in a city where there is a large selection of good bookstores, or you have a bookstore in your community with a good bookstore owner, you are very fortunate. Bookstore owners buy books that they feel their general clientele will buy. That means if you are looking for a special writing reference book, they may not have it in the store. You will have to ask them to order it for you. Most bookstores are happy to do that for you; it just means you have to wait for your book. You don't have to pay for the book until it comes into the store.

If you want to special-order a book, always go to the bookstore prepared with the name of the book, the author, the publisher, and the date and place it was published. You can ask the bookstore owner or clerk if there are any new books in your favorite genre. You can also ask them to help you find writing reference books.

Look for books in your particular genre, and preferably

from a variety of cultures. If you already have a home library, perhaps look at buying some classics. (An easy way to look for the classics in the English language will be to look under the Penguin label in most bookstores.)

If you have a birthday or special holiday on which you are given a present, it is a good idea to ask for unusual dictionaries, reference books, and anthologies, which may normally be out of your price range.

Scheduling Writing Time

If you have come up with your own writing timetable, inform your parents if you would like their support. For example, if you have household duties, perhaps you can swap evenings with one of your brothers or sisters. Or, if you have a heavy homework burden that has to be done to a strict timetable, and you can't see how to fit in two hours of writing a week, try asking your parents what they would do. Perhaps they will see a solution where you can't.

A Computer

If you are trying to write a long novel and don't have a computer that you can use either at home or school, set up a regular writing schedule and see if you can produce enough writing to convince your parents to help you get access to one.

FAMILY

My parents always encouraged me to read. Every now and then I would think, gee, wouldn't it be terrific if I had a friend to talk to about the stars, but there wasn't one.

Carl Sagan

Thankfully, writing appears to be one of those careers that parents can't push their children towards. When have you ever heard someone's parents say, "Gee, I wish my daughter would become a writer!" (I've yet to hear it! In fact, I never heard MY parents say it!)

One of the nice things about writing is that it really depends upon the initiative and talent of the individual. It is also what makes it so satisfying to actually succeed as a writer! At the same time, there is tremendous potential for young writers who are clear on how to enroll their parents in supporting them in various parts of their writing career.

I must admit I never made many requests of my parents or relatives because I didn't really know how they could help. But now I understand how parents and young writers can work effectively together. The following is a list of ideas you can do with your parents or relatives. Think about those that would appeal to you and that would work with your own parents and/or relatives. Then put the steps into motion to actually have some of them there for support.

Locating Artistic Relatives

Ask your parents if you have any relatives who are working in or have a strong love of the arts. You may find no one, in which case you'll have to use another network. But you may luck out, and find yourself sitting on a gold mine. (While I was at Sussex University in England, I was only miles away from my aunt, a syndicated columnist; my cousin, a playwright; and my cousin-in-law, an independent documentary producer who keeps his Emmy in his bathroom! It never even occurred to me to think of talking to them until I was much older.)

You may be surprised to find there is someone in your family besides yourself (an uncle? an older cousin?) who shares your love of books and writing.

Attend Author Readings Together

If one of your relatives also has an interest in writing, you can go together and listen to readings. Readings in public libraries by authors either are free or have a charge of a small entrance fee. They are a great way to meet authors and hear about their experiences. If you are into building an autographed copy library, the author's books are usually for sale at the event.

Finding Professional Coaching

Your parents may be willing to help you find writing workshops, or even a writer who is willing to coach you on an individual basis. They may be happy to send you to a summer writing camp or even help you put together the money to attend one—especially if there is nothing else for you to attend to improve your writing during the year.

Celebrating Special Days

In your own country and state or province, there are special days and weeks celebrating writing. See what special days you can find in your community. Your librarian should be able to help you. For example, in Canada, there is National Book Week in April. Also, P.E.N. International celebrates International Writers Day every year.

FEEDBACK ON YOUR WRITING

Getting reactions to your writing from people who can give you honest, constructive criticism, along with praise and support is extremely important to budding young authors. Following are some varied sources for this support network.

Mentors

"For most of my life I have dreamed of becoming a writer. In my teenage years, I gazed upon the likes of Gordon Korman and Lee J. Hindle (both had major publishing success as teenagers) with considerable admiration. . . . Oh, sure, I had a small handful of teachers along the way who urged me to continue, and my parents have always stood by my ideals, but nothing BIG happened. You probably know what I mean. I'm talking about the talent scout who meets a young Gretzky after a little league hockey game, telling him, 'You could go far, my boy! You've got what it takes!'"

The feelings of Derek Schraner are not unusual for young writers. Finding a mentor can be a wonderful solution to this dilemma.

A mentor is an adult who can help young people develop in a particular career area. Mentors for young writers can be teachers, professors, parents, and other writers. Here are a few ideas on how to work with other authors, teachers, and librarians.

You must feel safe with a mentor. It is your writing that is being developed, not somebody's thoughts on writing being forced upon you. You should feel that you are being coached to develop your own style. For example: How do the words sound to you? Do they sound strong enough to you?

You must feel you are getting honest feedback. For example, is your mentor giving you an honest estimate of how long it will take for a piece of writing to be developed into publishable material, or even to get published? Most of the short stories I see may be ready after a month's hard work, and a novel may take anywhere from six months to a year, depending on the manuscript and how much time the young writer can put into it.

Author Visits

If you actually have a chance to meet an author, you want to be prepared. Put together a list of questions you would like answered, and think seriously about what sort of feedback you would like on your writing—if, and only if, the author has time to look at it.

Authors are usually invited to schools and libraries to: a) give a reading from their work or b) do a writing workshop. While you might like them to read your whole novel at the workshop, it is not fair to expect them to do so. So what can you do to make the best of this visit?

First, find out from your teacher or the person planning the visit if the author will have time *during the workshop* to give you feedback on a particular piece of writing you are working on or have finished.

Second, if you have a piece of writing you would like them to read, read it through yourself and get a *real* estimate of how long it would take the author to read. If it will take the author one or two minutes to read, you may be in luck of having some feedback during the actual session. For example, one or two poems will work well. If it is going to take the author anywhere from ten minutes to half an hour to read, guess what? You guessed it! Impossible! So what do you do? Highlight one section of one or two pages you actually want feedback on. Or come up with your own idea, but watch the time limitations!

Three, if you are handing in pages of a story, the first question the author may ask you is, "What is your story about?" The author is not asking you to recite your story from beginning to end or to recite a complicated plot outline in fifteen minutes.

It is therefore wise to prepare a *very* short, precise summary of your story. Condense your story to three or four sentences. Make sure it takes less than a minute. Practice saying it to yourself in the mirror. Make sure you have got it down perfect.

For example, at the front of the book *Matilda* by Roald Dahl, the publisher put a brief summary of the book: "Matilda applied her untapped mental powers to rid the school of the evil, child-hating head-mistress, Miss Turnbull, to restore her nice teacher, Miss Honey, to financial security." Now those of you familiar with *Matilda* will know this is a very brief outline. But you know? It works.

Four, feedback. Be clear about what it is you want to know from the author. Try not to show a piece to an author simply to get assurance that you have talent. If you want to share a piece so that they enjoy reading it, fine. If you want help with a technical problem—somehow your description doesn't seem to work in a particular place or the dialogue falls flat—that is fine too.

Finally, if you have a tendency to get shy or nervous when talking to someone about your writing, remember that authors, poets, illustrators, etc., are visiting your school, library, or community because they care very much about stories and books.

Writers-in-Residence and Private Coaching

Aspiring writers do need exposure to authors. In some states, provinces, and counties, there are programs where you can actually take a manuscript in to an author and get feedback on it. Usually, the programs are done through libraries or universities, and are called "writer-in-the-libraries" or "writer-in-residence." Ask your librarian if she knows of a program that is coming to your library.

The other option is to look for an author who works well with young writers, and ask them to coach you on a private basis for a fee. While this system is well in place with music (in particular, piano teachers), the idea of a private writing coach is still news to most young writers, parents, and teachers. If you have liked the author and he lives in your community, you can go home and tell your parents, and perhaps you can negotiate a small fee with the author to read your material and give you constructive criticism.

If you can't find that, then try to attend young writers' workshops or intensive camps, where it is possible to get feedback on longer pieces of work. Working with a professional writer, whether at a summer camp, at a workshop, or on an individual basis, can be a wonderful experience.

Teachers and Librarians

Teachers and librarians can both be important sources of support. Teachers, particularly in English, can give you the flexibility to use your creative writing assignments for actual writing publication assignments. Librarians can be a wonderful source of knowledge regarding interesting books and organizations.

QUESTIONS ON WRITING IN THE CLASSROOM

Question: My teacher has asked for a 1,000 word story. I want to do a 2,000 word story because that is the required word count for a publication's contest I want to enter.

Answer: There are two possibilities here. You can take the word count to be an important disciplining action and see how you can write a "tighter" story. Or, you can explain to your teacher why you want to do a longer story and see if you can get special permission. If you can't, you'll just have to do the story on your own time.

Question: When my teacher edits my work, it ends up being totally changed, and I don't like it any more.

Answer: Talk to your teacher and explain why it is important that you keep your story a particular way. This is good practice because an editor at a publishing house may do the exact same thing to you.

Question: My teacher didn't believe a piece of writing was my own. (Let's hope this one doesn't happen to you.)

Answer: Always keep all your drafts and notes as you work. If there is any question, show these to your parents and explain the problem. They can accompany you to school.

_____ACTIVITIES

Classics

I've read portions of *The Closing of the American Mind*, as well as *Madame Bovary* and Machiavelli's *The Prince*. I think I'm discovering a world I didn't know existed.

John, age seventeen

The purpose of the activity is to encourage you to read and build your own library of the classics.

Here are three of my favorite classics: Stendhal's *The Red and the Black*, Flaubert's *Madame Bovary*, and George Eliot's *Silas Marner*.

Put aside some time to read one of the three titles above. Then, explore the other classics and come up with your own top three favorites.

Compare your favorites with a friend's favorites. What interested you in the book? What was fascinating about the period of time the book was written in? Do good books really seem timeless? For example, are there really some of the same problems no matter how civilization progresses?

Linking Up

This is a partial list of professional writing organizations by country (Australia, Canada, United Kingdom, and United States). Membership in these organizations usually requires some publishing track record. Those organizations with membership categories open to unpublished writers are marked with a ▲ symbol.

They produce excellent material on contracts, current markets, local writing seminars, grants, awards, etc. This material is available for a small fee. Please do not ask the staff of these organizations for editorial advice or answers to questions you can easily find with a bit of research yourself.

Read through the list pertaining to your country and find

one organization that you would like to know more about. Write to the organization requesting general information about membership, publications, and workshops for young writers in your area. When you receive the information, place the requirements for membership in a safe place.

Read through the list of publications and see if there are any of interest to you. You can also take the list in to your teacher/librarian and see if they would like to order a copy. You can also see if there are any local workshops in your area.

It is important to remember that most of these organizations will help you—even if you are not a member—to understand your first publishing contract.

Australia

Australian Writers' Guild, Ltd.
60 Kellett Street
Kings Cross Sydney, NSW 2011
(02) 3577888

Poetry Society of Australia
P.O. Box N110
Grosvenor Street
Sydney, NSW 2000

The Australian Society of Authors Ltd.
P.O. Box 450
Milsons Point, NSW 2061
(02) 927235

Canada

▲ Canadian Society of Children's Authors, Illustrators and
Performers
P.O. Box 280
Station L
Toronto, Ontario M6E 4Z2
300 professional members and 600 friends. $15.00 membership as a "friend" (not published) entitles you to a quarterly newsletter. Meets monthly in Toronto, Ontario and Vancouver, British Columbia.

The League of Canadian Poets
24 Ryerson Avenue
Toronto, Ontario M5T 2P3
(416) 363-5074

The Writers' Union of Canada
24 Ryerson Avenue
Toronto, Ontario M5T 2P3
(416) 868-6914

The Periodical Writers' Association of Canada
24 Ryerson Avenue
Toronto, Ontario M5T 2P3
(416) 868-6913

The Playwrights Union of Canada
54 Wolseley Street
Toronto, Ontario M5T 1A5
(416) 947-0201

ACTRA
Writer's Guild
2239 Yonge Street
Toronto, Ontario M4S 2B5
(416) 489-1311

United Kingdom

The Writers' Guild of Great Britain
430 Edgware Road
London W2 1EH

The Society of Authors
84 Drayton Gardens
London SW10 9SB

The Poetry Society
21 Earls Court Square
London SW5 9DE

For a complete listing of professional associations in Great Britain, refer to *The Writer's Handbook* (Macmillan/ Pen).

United States

▲ The Society of Children's Book Writers
P.O. Box 296
Mar Vista Station
Los Angeles, CA 90066

The Authors' Guild, Inc.
300 West 42nd Street
29th Floor
New York, NY 10036

Other Countries

Refer to "Literary Associations" in *International Literary Marketplace*. New York: R.R. Bowker, 1990. (Published annually.)

Reading

Bloom, Allan. *The Closing of the American Mind*. New York: Simon & Schuster, 1987.

Chapter Three gives excellent ideas about what classics to read.

Henderson, Kathy. *Market Guide for Young Writers, Third Edition*. Crozet, Virginia: Betterway Publications, 1990.

Gives information on linking up electronically with other young writers.

Nolan, Christopher. *Under The Eye of the Clock*. Oxford: Isis, 1988.

An autobiography of how Christopher overcame some of the hardships of being severely handicapped to become a highly-respected poet. Shows how working with one's parents and friends can really help your career.

Reilly, Jill. *Is There A Mentorship In Your Future?*. Ohio: Ohio Psychology Press, 1991.

Discusses finding out about what it takes to find and work with a mentor.

Writing is one of those things that stays with you your whole life. When your mom's in labour, the expecting family is pacing back and forth—and reading. You spend half of your life in school, the most important part of your life, and what do you do—read and write. As you grow older, filling out job applications, driver's license, reports, etc., what do you do—read and write. So when you sit there, hunched over and brain-fried, asking 'Why should I break my back?' just think. Since the beginning of time, writing has been the center of civilization.

Steve, age fifteen

Appendix

The International Young Authors' Camps

The International Young Authors' Camps is an international network of private camps designed specifically to provide the best training possible for highly-motivated young writers. The camps are held on an annual basis for a period of approximately one week in different locations around the world. A cost to attend is involved. Selection is based on submission of a writing sample.

The Canadian Young Authors' Camp, located in Haliburton, Ontario, was established in 1989 and currently attracts an international staff of authors as well as young writers from across North America.

Future country sites include the United States and Australia.

For details of the camp nearest to you and scheduled dates, contact:

The International Young Authors' Camps
Suite 4-407
264 Queens Quay West
Toronto, Ontario
CANADA M5J 1B5

ABOUT THE AUTHOR

Janet Grant is the founder and director of the International Young Authors' Camps.

Born in Toronto, Canada in 1957, she graduated from the University of Sussex, England, with a Honours B.A. in English Literature in the School of Cultural and Community Studies. Returning to Canada in 1980, she led corporate workshops in British Columbia, becoming one of North America's youngest corporate writing consultants.

At age twenty-six, she established her own business in Toronto, leading corporate and private workshops, as well as a private consulting practice for empowering teenagers to reach their academic goals. During this time, she created an innovative methodolgy for developing talent in teenagers, as well as authoring eight books for children, teenagers, and educators. She also established an annual summer camp for young writers across North America — the Canadian Young Authors' Camp in Haliburton, Ontario. In 1991, Janet E. Grant founded the International Young Authors' Camps.

Index